**Adopted: April 6, 2007**  **Released: April 25, 2007**

By the Commission: Chairman Martin, Commissioners Copps, Tate, and McDowell issuing separate statements; Commissioner Adelstein approving in part, concurring in part, and issuing a statement.

## TABLE OF CONTENTS

APPENDIX: List of Commenters

## I.    INTRODUCTION

1.     Television is an integral part of the lives of American families.  An average American household has the television set turned on 8 hours and 11 minutes daily,[1] and children watch on average between two and four hours of television every day.[2]  Depending on their age, one to two thirds of children have televisions in their bedrooms.[3]  By the time most children begin the first grade, they will have spent the equivalent of three school years in front of the television set.[4]

---

[1] *See* Nielsen Media Research (for the 2004-2005 season).

[2] *Id.* Other researchers have found that children ages 0-6 watch an average of one hour of television a day.  *See* Kaiser Family Foundation, *Zero to Six: Electronic Media in the Lives of Infants, Toddlers, and Preschoolers* (Fall 2003) ("*Kaiser Kids and Media Report*"); *see also*, Harris Interactive, *Born to Be Wired: A New Media Landscape Comes of Age*, *at* http://us.i1.yimg.com/us.yimg.com/i/promo/btbw_2003/btbw_execsum.pdf (finding that 13-24 year olds watch, on average, 13.6 hours of television per week).

[3] *See, e.g., Kaiser Kids and Media Report* at 7 (stating that 30% of children 0-3 years old have a television in their bedroom and 43% of children 4-6 have a television in their bedroom); *Id.* at 20; Knowledge Networks/SRI, *How*

(continued....)

2.	Violent content in television programming has been a matter of private and governmental concern and discussion almost from the beginning of television broadcasting.[5] A broad range of television programming aired today contains such content, including, for example, cartoons, dramatic series, professional sports such as boxing, news coverage, and nature programs. The public is concerned about the amount of violent television programming available to children, with many urging action to restrict such content.[6]

3.	It is within this context that the Commission received a request from thirty-nine members of the U.S. House of Representatives asking us to undertake an inquiry on television violence.[7] In response, the Commission issued a *Notice of Inquiry* ("*NOI*")[8] in this proceeding, seeking public input on a variety of matters tied to the issue of violent television content. The Commission has received hundreds of filings from interested parties and individuals.

4.	The House members asked the Commission to solicit comment on three essential issues:

- What are the negative effects on children caused by the cumulative viewing of excessively violent programming?

- What are the constitutional limits on the government's ability to restrict the broadcast of excessively violent programming when children are likely to be a significant or substantial part of the viewing audience? In particular, could

---

(...continued from previous page)
*Children Use Media Technology* (2003), *at* http://www.sri.knowledgenetworks.com (finding that 6 out of 10 8-17-year-old children had televisions in their bedrooms, and 1 out of 3 of the same group have cable television).

[4] *See Children's Television Obligations of Digital Television Broadcasters,* Second Order on Reconsideration and Second Report and Order, 21 FCC Rcd 11065, 11066 (citations omitted).

[5] *See, e.g.,* U.S. Congress, House Committee on Interstate and Foreign Commerce, *Investigation of Radio and Television Programs*, 82nd Cong., 2d Sess. (1952); National Commission on the Causes and Prevention of Violence (1969); Surgeon General's Scientific Advisory Commission on Television and Social Behavior (1972); *Report on the Broadcast of Violent, Indecent, and Obscene Material*, 51 F.C.C.2d 418 (1975); Federal Trade Commission, *Marketing Violent Entertainment to Children: A Review of Self-Regulation and Industry Practices in the Motion Picture, Music Recording & Electronic Games Industries* (2000) ("*2000 FTC Report*"); and *Youth Violence: A Report of the Surgeon General* (2001) ("*2001 SG Report*").

[6] *See New Poll Finds Escalating Violence in Children's TV Now a Crisis for Parents*, http://media.prnewswire.com/en/jsp/main.jsp?resourceid=3051704, October 10, 2005 (reporting that poll conducted by the American Business Research Corporation found that nine out of ten parents with children aged 1-6 believed that violence in children's programming had a serious negative impact); *see also* Comments of Jennifer Christenson (urging FCC to "work to lessen, even better—end violent programming on television."); Carmen Hank (calling on the FCC to "restrict the amount of violence shown on any TV program by any station."); and Aaron Pavkov (asking the FCC "to reign [sic] in violent television programming."). On the other hand, several commenters state that the Commission should not regulate television violence and that parents should be ultimately responsible for what content their children can access. *See* Comments of Noelle Stout (opining that individuals should "make their own choices based on their sensitivity to violence rather than the government trying to define a common law for all."); Comments of Chris Spedaliere (stating that it should be the "parents' responsibility to tell their children what they can or cannot watch and the government should have no part in it at all.").

[7] Letter from Hon. Joe Barton, Chairman, U.S. House of Representatives Committee on Energy and Commerce, *et. al.*, to Hon. Michael K. Powell, Chairman, FCC (Mar. 5, 2004) ("House Commerce Committee Letter"). On March 14, 2005, Senators Rockefeller and Hutchison introduced *The Indecent and Gratuitous and Excessively Violent Programming Control Act of 2005* which addressed related issues. *See* Cong. Rec. S2649 (Mar. 14, 2005).

[8] *Violent Television Programming and Its Impact on Children*, 19 FCC Rcd 14394 (2004).

television violence regulations, including possible time channeling requirements, be narrowly tailored to the governmental interests they are intended to serve?

- Is it in the public interest for the government to adopt a definition of "excessively violent programming that is harmful to children," and could the government formulate and implement such a definition in a constitutional manner?

5.    *Summary.*  In the *NOI*, the Commission sought comment on the relationship between media violence and aggression in children.  In this *Report*, we find that there is deep concern among many American parents and health professionals regarding harm from viewing violence in media.  We also agree with the views of the Surgeon General that there is strong evidence that exposure to violence in the media can increase aggressive behavior in children, at least in the short term.  In the *NOI*, the Commission sought comment on proposals aimed at regulating violent television content, such as a "safe harbor" period similar to the one in place for indecent broadcast content.  In this *Report*, we recognize that violent content is a protected form of speech under the First Amendment, but note that the government interests at stake, such as protecting children from excessively violent television programming, are similar to those which have been found to justify other content-based regulations.  In the *NOI*, the Commission asked questions concerning the adequacy of current program blocking technology and the effectiveness of the TV ratings system in helping parents control access to violent programming.  In this *Report*, we find that although the V-chip and TV ratings system appear useful in the abstract, they are not effective at protecting children from violent content for a number of reasons.  In particular, we find that the TV ratings system has certain weaknesses that prevent parents from screening out much programming that they find objectionable.  In the *NOI*, the Commission asked how the government might define "violence" for regulatory purposes.  In this *Report*, we recognize the difficulties associated with drafting a concise and legally sustainable definition of violence for regulatory purposes, but we suggest an approach that Congress may want to consider in crafting a definition.  Finally, we note our conclusion that, given the findings in this report, action should be taken to address violent programming and suggest that Congress could implement a time-channeling solution that would more effectively protect children from violent programming and/or mandate other forms of consumer choice that would better support parents' efforts to safeguard their children from exposure to violent programming.

## II.    THE EFFECTS OF VIEWING VIOLENT TELEVISION PROGRAMMING ON CHILDREN

6.    We agree with the views of the Surgeon General and find that, on balance, research provides strong evidence that exposure to violence in the media can increase aggressive behavior in children, at least in the short term.[9]  Over the course of several decades, considerable research has been undertaken to examine television's impact on children's learning and behavior.[10]  Three types of studies

---

[9] *See infra* ¶ 12.  We note that most of these studies examined both broadcast and cable television, and some studies also included other media, including films and video games.

[10]  There has been some dispute regarding the amount of research in the field of television violence and aggression.  *Compare, e.g.,* American Academy of Pediatrics, *Media Violence,* 108 Pediatrics 1222, 1223 (Nov. 2001) ("[m]ore than 3500 research studies have examined the association between media violence and violent behavior; all but 18 have shown a positive relationship") *with* Donnerstein, *Mass Media Violence: Thoughts on the Debate,* 22 Hofstra L. Rev. 827, 828 (1994) ("There are not three thousand studies on television violence.  There are perhaps three thousand studies on television.  But there probably are approximately two hundred or two hundred and fifty studies directly related to violence in the media.").  Craig Anderson states that most of the discrepancies in the claims about how many studies have been conducted are the result of differing definitions of what constitutes a "study."  Some scholars include every publication that discusses media violence in scientific journals or books, regardless of whether or not it reports new data.  Anderson states that this leads to the very high numbers of studies cited. Other researchers include in their definition only original empirical studies of the effects of exposure to television violence

(continued....)

are generally described in the literature: (1) field experiments in which subjects are shown video programming and their short-term post-viewing behavior is monitored by researchers; (2) cross-sectional studies involving samples of individuals whose conduct is correlated with the amount and type of their television viewing; and (3) longitudinal studies that survey the same group of individuals at different times over many years to determine the effects of television viewing on subsequent behavior.[11] Through these studies, scholars have attempted to establish a cause-and-effect relationship between viewing violent content and subsequent aggression in children.

7.      The researchers have focused on three possible harmful effects: (1) increased antisocial behavior, including imitations of aggression or negative interactions with others, (2) increased desensitization to violence, and (3) increased fear of becoming a victim of violence.[12] Researchers have theorized that children's viewing of violent television programming may affect later behavior in three ways: (1) through observing schemas about a hostile world, (2) through scripts for social problem solving that focus on aggression, and (3) through normative beliefs that aggression is acceptable. Alternatively, exposure to violent programming may desensitize the child's innate negative emotional response to violence, thus making aggressive acts easier to commit or tolerate.[13] While the Commission sought evidence relating to such research, very little new information on the issue was submitted into the record of this proceeding.

8.      Some studies find evidence of a cause-and-effect relationship between viewing televised violence by children and aggression or other changes in the behavior of the children on both a short-term and a longer-term basis.[14] For example, Craig Anderson, a professor and former chair of the Psychology Department at Iowa State University who has conducted and published numerous "media harms" studies,[15] asserts that research on violent television, films, video games, and music reveals "unequivocal

---

(...continued from previous page)
on some form of aggressive behavior. Anderson states that this leads to a much lower number of reported studies. He states that even in this restrictive definition, there is room for ambiguity. Many published empirical articles that have original results (*i.e.*, results from new samples of participants) contain more than one study. Anderson states that, in any case, the number of independent, original studies is quite large, and the results are generally consistent in finding a positive relationship between television violence and aggression. Anderson Comments at 2-3.

[11] *See, e.g.*, Paik & Comstock, *Effect of Television Violence on Antisocial Behavior: A Meta-Analysis*, Communication Research 21:4, 516-46 (1994).

[12] *Third National TV Violence Study* at 5, 7 (Federman ed.) ("*Third National TV Violence Study Summary*"). This study involved media researchers at four universities and an oversight council and was funded by the National Cable Television Association (now the National Cable & Telecommunications Association). The study was not limited to broadcast television but also included non-broadcast program networks (including some premium channels, such as HBO).

[13] *See, e.g.*, Huesmann, *et. al.*, *Longitudinal Relations Between Children's Exposure to TV Violence and Their Aggressive and Violent Behavior in Young Adulthood: 1977-1992*, Developmental Psychology, Vol. 39, No. 2, 201-221 (2003) ("*Longitudinal Relations Study*") (examining the longitudinal relationship between television violence viewing at ages 6 to 10 and adult aggressive behavior about 15 years later for a sample growing up in the 1970s and 1980s and concluding that childhood exposure to media violence predicts young adult aggressive behavior for both males and females.).

[14] *See 2001 SG Report* at Appendix 4-B.

[15] *See, e.g.,* Gentile, D.A., & Anderson, C.A., *Violent Video Games: Effects of Youth and Public Policy Implications,* Chapter in N. Dowd, D. G. Singer, & R. F. Wilson (Eds.), *Handbook of Children, Culture, and Violence,* 225-246 (2006); Carnagey, N. L., & Anderson, C.A., *The Effects of Reward and Punishment in Violent Video Games on Aggressive Affect, Cognition, and Behavior*, Psychological Science, 16, 882-889 (2005); Anderson, C.A., *An Update on the Effects of Violent Video Games,* Journal of Adolescence, 27, 113-122 (2004); Anderson, C.A., Berkowitz, L., Donnerstein, E., Huesmann, R.L., Johnson, J., Linz, D., Malamuth, N., & Wartella, E., *The Influence of Media Violence on Youth*, Psychological Science in the Public Interest, 4, 81-110 (2003).

evidence" that media violence increases the likelihood of aggressive and violent behavior in both immediate and long-term contexts.[16] According to his analyses and assessments, media violence produces short-term effects by "increasing physiological arousal and triggering an automatic tendency to imitate observed behaviors," and exposure to media violence leads to lasting aggressive behavior and desensitizes individuals to actual violence.[17] Anderson notes that, although certain characteristics of viewers (*e.g.*, identification with aggressive characters), social environments (*e.g.*, parental influences), and media content (*e.g.*, attractiveness of the portrayed perpetrator) can influence the degree to which media violence affects aggression, "no one is exempt from the deleterious effects of media violence."[18]

9.      Joanne Cantor, a professor at the University of Wisconsin-Madison, concurs and states that her research has found that children show higher levels of hostility after exposure to media violence - ranging from being in a "nasty mood" to an increased tendency to interpret a neutral comment or action as an attack.[19] She also asserts that her studies have found that media violence makes children fearful, a condition expressed as a general sense that the world is dangerous or through nightmares and other sleep disturbances.[20] In congressional testimony, Dale Kunkel, a professor at the University of Arizona and an expert in the field of media violence, stated, "it is well established by a compelling body of scientific evidence that television violence poses a risk of harmful effects for the child-viewer."[21] The Children's Media Policy Coalition ("CMPC"), a group consisting of several health and child advocacy groups such as the American Academy of Pediatrics, argues that certain critics[22] of the "cause and effect theory" have mischaracterized the numerous studies by limiting the question to whether or not "watching violence on television causes watchers to commit violence."[23] According to CPMC, the conclusion is not that media violence is the sole cause of aggression in children, but that the depiction of violence in media is one factor potentially contributing to the risk that children will suffer a number of harmful effects. Thus, there is a considerable research community that has studied television's effects on children's health over an extended period of time and defends the proposition that viewing this programming has adverse consequences for the child audience.

10.      The *Notice of Inquiry* in this proceeding referenced two recent significant efforts to summarize the state of the evidence regarding the effects of televised violence on children.   A review of

---

[16] *See* Anderson Comments at 1-2, citing Anderson, *et. al.*, *The Influence of Media Violence on Youth*, Psychological Science in the Public Interest, Vol. 4, No. 3 (Dec. 2003) (concluding that exposure to media violence [movies, television, music, and videogames] has a statistically significant association with aggression and violence among youth).

[17] *Id.*

[18] Anderson Comments at 2; *see also* Children's and Media Policy Coalition Comments at 4 (agreeing that children who are exposed to violent programming face a higher risk of suffering from harmful consequences). Jerry Kroth, an Associate Professor for Graduate Studies in Counseling Psychology, Education, and Pastoral Ministries, at Santa Clara University, submitted comments purporting to demonstrate that several dozen youth deaths can be attributed to individuals copying media depictions of antisocial behavior. *See* Kroth & Forrest, *Psychology Underground: From Politically Correct Orthodoxies to a New Century of Inquiry*, Academic Renewal Press (2001).

[19] Joanne Cantor has studied the effects of media violence for more than 30 years.  She has published several scholarly articles on the subject, was a senior researcher on the *National Television Violence Study*, and has testified numerous times before the U.S. House and Senate, as well as before the FCC.

[20] Cantor Comments at 1 (internal citations omitted).

[21] Testimony of Dale Kunkel before the United States House of Representatives, Committee on Energy and Commerce, September 13, 2004.

[22] Such critics include the American Civil Liberties Union ("ACLU") (*see* Comments at 1); Media Associations (*see* Comments at 13); and the National Association of Broadcasters ("NAB") (*see* Comments at 7-8).

[23] CMPC Reply Comments at 2-3.

the scientific research, which appears as part of the Federal Trade Commission's report on *Marketing Violent Entertainment to Children*, summarized the research as follows:

> A majority of the investigations into the impact of media violence on children find that there is a high *correlation* between exposure to media violence and aggressive and at times violent behavior. In addition, a number of research efforts report that exposure to media violence is correlated with increased acceptance of violent behavior in others, as well as an exaggerated perception of the amount of violence in society. Regarding *causation*, however, the studies appear to be less conclusive. Most researchers and investigators agree that exposure to media violence alone does not cause a child to commit a violent act, and that it is not the sole, or even necessarily the most important, factor contributing to youth aggression, anti-social attitudes, and violence. Although a consensus among researchers exists regarding the empirical relationships, significant differences remain over the interpretation of these associations and their implications for public policy.[24]

Others agree that while studies show a correlation, a clear causal link has not been conclusively proven.[25] More recently, researchers at Boston Children's Hospital report that violent shows might teach and encourage aggressive behavior in children, which in turn isolates them from their peers. Like the *FTC Report*, the study shows a correlation, but does not prove causation.[26]

11.     A Joint Statement by the American Academy of Pediatrics, American Academy of Child & Adolescent Psychiatry, American Academy of Family Physicians, American Medical Association, American Psychological Association, and American Psychiatric Association summarized the effects of violence as follows:

- Viewing violence can lead to emotional desensitization towards violence in real life.
- Children exposed to violent programming at a young age have a higher tendency for violent and aggressive behavior later in life than children who are not so exposed.
- Children exposed to violence are more likely to assume that acts of violence are acceptable behavior.
- Viewing violence increases fear of becoming a victim of violence, with a resultant increase in self-protective behaviors and a mistrust of others.[27]

12.     The United States Surgeon General's *Youth Violence: A Report of the Surgeon General* also summarized the research in this area:

> In sum, a diverse body of research provides strong evidence that exposure to violence in the media can increase children's aggressive behavior in the short term. Some studies suggest that long-term effects exist, and there are strong theoretical reasons why this is the case. But

---

[24] *2000 FTC Report* at Appendix A (footnotes omitted) (emphasis added).

[25] *See* Michael Shimanovsky, *Influences Exerted on the Child Viewer When Exposed to Violent Imagery in Television and Print Advertising*, Journal of Evolutionary Psychology (October 2006).

[26] *See* Sandra Boodman, *Solo Viewing, Bad Endings; Watching Violent TV May Cost Kids Friends*, Washington Post, April 11, 2006, at F1.

[27] American Academy of Pediatrics, et. al, *Joint Statement on the Impact of Entertainment Violence on Children, Congressional Public Health Summit* (July 2000).

many questions remain regarding the short- and long-term effects of media violence, especially on violent behavior. Despite considerable advances in research, it is not yet possible to describe accurately how much exposure, of what types, for how long, at what ages, for what types of children, or in what types of settings will predict violent behavior in adolescents and adults.[28]

13.     Research since these reports were issued seems to be consistent with much of the prior research. One more recent effort, subsequent to the *Surgeon General* and *Federal Trade Commission Reports*, attempts to carefully track a specific child population from 1977 to 1992 in order to correlate viewing of violent television with subsequent aggression.[29] This longitudinal study supports the oft-stated conclusion that the effect of childhood exposure to media violence lasts into adulthood and increases aggressive behavior. While acknowledging that "longitudinal non-experimental data do not provide a strong test of causation," the paper concludes that the structural models used

> show that for both boys and girls, habitual early exposure to TV violence is predictive of more aggression by them later in life independent of their own initial childhood aggression, their own intellectual capabilities, their social status as measured by their parents' education or their father's occupation, their parents' TV viewing habits (including violence viewing), and their parents' rejection, nurturance, and punishment of them in childhood.[30]

14.     Two additional specific areas of research warrant particular mention. As was noted in the *NOI*, magnetic resonance imaging ("MRI") brain mapping techniques are being developed to measure directly specific changes in brain function as a consequence of children's exposure to media violence.[31] The Center for Successful Parenting ("CSP") commented that it had directly sponsored academic research to generate objective data concerning the effects of violent media on the development of children and adolescents. CSP described this research as focused on the relationship and association between the amount of media violence exposure and pre-frontal cortical brain function as well as aggressive behavior. The accrued data and findings are based on functional brain activity using MRI brain-mapping techniques. These studies indicated that exposure to media violence directly affects the pre-frontal cortex,

---

[28] *2001 SG Report* at Appendix 4-B.

[29] *See Longitudinal Relations Study,* at 201-221 (2003). There have been other studies attempting to show that the introduction of television in society is linked to a subsequent increase in criminal activity. *See* Centerwell, *Exposure to Television as a Risk Factor for Violence,* Am. J. of Epidemiology Vol. 129 at 643-652 (1989) (introduction of television in South Africa in the 1970s purportedly linked to subsequent violent activity in that country); Centerwall, *Exposure to Television as a Cause of Violence,* Public Communication and Behavior, at 1-58 (Comstock, ed. Academic Press 1989) (stating the same). However, these studies have come under heavy criticism as being poorly designed and lacking in scientific value. *See, e.g.,* Wilson, *Connections Among Television, Guns and Violence,* presented at the Manhattan Institute for Policy Research–1998 Annual James Q. Wilson Lecture, available at http://www manhattan-institute.org/html/jqw1998.htm; Rhodes, *The Media Violence Myth,* available at http://www.abffe.com/myth1 htm; Fowles, *Missing Link–The Bum Rap Against TV Violence,* available at http://www reason.com/0103/fe.jf missing.shtml.

[30] *Longitudinal Relations Study*, at 216-217.

[31] Wang, *et. al., Effects of Violent Media on Adolescents With Disruptive Behavior Disorder As Compared to Control Subjects: MRI Activation Patterns in Frontal Lobe,* paper presented a the 88th Scientific Assembly and Annual Meeting of the Radiological Society of North America, December 2002. *See also* Mathews, *et. al., Brain Activation and Violent Video Games,* presented at the 2002 Radiological Society of North America annual meeting; Surface, *Imaging Video Violence,* Radiology Today, March 31, 2003.

an area of the brain involved in learning and behavior.[32] CSP's website describes the findings and conclusions of the research. Among other things, the researchers found that "[n]ormal adolescents who had a higher level of violent media exposure had reduced levels of cognitive brain function" and that "[a]ggressive behavior can be associated with higher levels of violent media exposure," and "[a]ggressive adolescents show less cognitive brain activity than normal adolescents do." The researchers concluded that "[t]here is a correlation between the degree of exposure to television/movie violence and violence in video games and normal brain function."[33]

      15.     The second area of new research involves differentiating among types of violent programming content and the context in which violence appears. Many television violence studies have used a single definition of violence that does not differentiate among types of violence or how violence is depicted in context. A more recent effort has paid greater attention to context. A study performed by Barbara Wilson, a professor at the University of Illinois, and her research colleagues identified eight contextual factors thought to be important in determining the likely impact of violence on both child and adult viewers.[34] Further research by Wilson indicates that programs targeted to children contain more violence than do other types of programming. The violence itself is just as likely to be glamorized in children's as in non-children's shows, but it is even more sanitized and more likely to be trivialized. According to Wilson, these patterns heighten the risk of viewers learning aggression and becoming desensitized from such portrayals.[35]

      16.     Others argue, however, that children are not necessarily harmed by exposure to television violence or that the research on the topic is flawed or inconclusive.[36] The Media Coalition, a group of trade associations representing book and magazine publishers, along with movie, recording and video manufacturers and retailers, disputes that research supports the conclusion that violence in the media causes actual violence. In support of this view, they contend that the existing research is inconclusive and that there is no correlation between media violence and actual crime statistics.[37] The Media Associations, a group consisting of advertising, broadcast, and television production entities, have examined the studies

---

[32] *See* CSP Comments at 1.

[33] http://www.sosparents.org/Brain%20Research%20Study.htm.

[34] These eight factors are: (1) the nature of the perpetrator, including in particular whether the perpetrator is attractive; (2) the motive or reason for the violence, including whether it is morally defensible or unjustified; (3) the presence of weapons; (4) whether the violence is extensive or graphic; (5) whether the violence seems realistic; (6) whether the violence is explicitly rewarded or goes unpunished; (7) the consequences of violence for the victim; (8) whether the violence is portrayed as humorous. Wilson, Smith, Potter, Kunkel, Linz, Colvin, and Donnerstein, *Violence in Children's Television Programming: Assessing the Risks*, Journal of Communications, Mar. 2003. This study investigated the nature and extent of violence contained in television programming that targets children aged 12 and younger. The measures employed in this content analysis are grounded in previous experimental research that has identified contextual features that either diminish or enhance the risk of harmful effects associated with viewing violent portrayals. This report uses the database from the *National Television Violence Study* (Wilson et al., 1998), which involved an unusually large and representative sample of programming.

[35] *See* University of California, Santa Barbara *et al.*, *National Television Violence Study: Scientific Papers*, 1994-1995, I-35 (Mediascope, Inc. ed., 1996).

[36] *See* Andrew O'Hehir, *The Myth of Media Violence, at* http://www.salon.com/index.html, March 17, 2005 (critiquing research finding television violence is harmful to children). Some have also suggested that the real problem is not with particular shows but the fact that children are spending substantial amounts of time watching television. *See* Robinson, Wilde, Navracruz, Haydel, and Varady, *Effects of Reducing Children's Television and Video Game Use on Aggressive Behavior: A Randomized Controlled Trial*, Archives of Pediatrics & Adolescent Medicine, Vol 155, at 17-23 (2001) (reducing children's television viewing times, along with their use of electronic games, for six months reduces by half incidents of aggressive behavior).

[37] Media Coalition Comments at 5-6.

on media violence and assert that the literature does not support either the claim of a causal relationship between media violence and aggression or the proposition that exposure to violent media leads to desensitization.[38] The Media Associations assert that research findings often are mischaracterized, and, in some cases, reach conclusions that are the opposite of what has been reported. To support their claims, the Media Associations note that Jonathan Freedman, a professor at the University of Toronto and critic of the media violence cause-and-effect theory,[39] conducted a comprehensive review of all of the available research on this topic and concluded that "evidence does not support the hypothesis that exposure to film or television violence causes children or adults to be aggressive."[40]

17.     Freedman reviewed each relevant media violence study and classified it as: (1) supporting the causal hypothesis, (2) failing to support the causal hypothesis, or (3) yielding mixed results. Freedman reviewed laboratory experiments, field experiments, and longitudinal studies, finding problems with each method. For example, laboratory experiments are short term, involve only brief exposures to programs, use measures of aggression that are often questionable, and are conducted in an artificial environment, thereby increasing the effect of "experimenter demand."[41] Freedman considered field experiments to be the best test of the hypothesis because they are done in natural settings and therefore avoid many of the problems of the laboratory research.[42] According to Freedman, the fact that the field experiments produced negative results for the causal hypothesis is a strong indication that laboratory results are not due to the direct effect of violent media.[43] Freedman concluded that the evidence from longitudinal studies provides little support for the causal hypothesis and, instead, could be interpreted as evidence against that hypothesis.[44] But CMPC attacks Freedman's conclusions, stating that he has never conducted empirical research on the effects of media violence. Their comments also note that Freedman has been paid by parties (such as the motion picture industry) with a vested interest in the outcome of such studies.[45]

---

[38] Media Associations Comments at 13; NAB Comments at 7.

[39] Jonathan Freedman is currently the vice-president and principal of the University of Toronto Scarborough. He has written several scholarly works on the flaws inherent in media violence research over the course of his 40-year career, including *Media Violence and Its Effect on Aggression: Assessing the Scientific Evidence*, University of Toronto Press (2002); *Violence in the Mass Media and Violence in Society: The Link is Unproven*, 12(11) The Harvard Mental Health Letter 4-6 (1996); *Viewing Violence Does Not Make People More Aggressive*, 22 Hofstra Law Review 833 (1994); *Television Violence and Aggression: What the Evidence Shows*, 8 Applied Social Psychology Annual 144 (1988); *Television Violence and Aggression: A Rejoinder*, 100 Psychological Bulletin, 372 (1986); *Effect of Television Violence on Aggressiveness*, 96 Psychological Bulletin, 227 (1984).

[40] Media Associations Comments at 13.

[41] Media Associations Comments at 12-13; *see also* Michael Males Comments at 5 (noting that "laboratory studies of psychological and sociological phenomena are weak tools, prone to unpredictable biases," such as experimenter effects).

[42] Field experiments are experiments done in natural settings, as opposed to a laboratory. These experiments show the subjects programs in the subjects' homes or classrooms and observe behavior in the school playground or equivalent setting.

[43] Media Associations Comments at 15.

[44] *Id.* at 16, 20; *see also* Media Institute Comments at 4 (stating that the Federal Trade Commission recently reviewed the body of scientific research in the area and found that most researchers agree that "exposure to media violence alone does not cause a child to commit a violent act" and that media violence "is not the sole, or even the most important, factor in contributing to youth aggression, anti-social attitudes, and violence"); *see also* ACLU Comments at 1-2 (citing the same).

[45] CMPC Reply Comments at 7-8.

18.     Michael Males, at the University of California-Santa Cruz,[46] critiques those studies that have reported a positive link or correlation between media violence and aggression in children. He asserts that there are a number of reasons why occasional positive results do not support the hypothesis that media violence has adverse real-world effects. First, he states that studies showing a "statistically significant" link between violent entertainment and aggressive behavior do not mean that the link exists for most, or even a substantial minority of, individuals. That is, "[s]ignificant" in the statistical sense "does not mean 'important;'" it means simply "not likely to happen just by chance."[47] Second, he states that researchers have used vastly different examples of violent content in the cartoons, film clips, or games that they study.[48] He concludes that generalizations about all violence from these differing examples are not trustworthy and fail to account for the many different contexts in which works of art or entertainment present violence. Third, he states that experimenters have not always made their nonviolent video clips equivalent to their violent ones with respect to other variables, such as general level of interest among children.[49] Fourth, he states that aggressive attitudes or "cognition" are not the same as aggressive behavior. Males asserts that proxies for aggression in lab experiments range from dubious (*e.g.*, making noise blasts; hitting "Bobo dolls;" "killing" characters in a video game) to ludicrous (*e.g.*, popping balloons).[50] Finally, he states that aggressive play, whether in a lab or in the real world, is far different from real aggression intended to hurt another person. According to Males, aggressive play provides a socially approved outlet for impulses that otherwise might take dangerous forms.[51]

19.     Another study, undertaken for the Government of New Zealand, reported that "[w]hat cannot be shown definitively is that television violence on its own is the cause of anti-social or violent behavior . . . [it] is one potentially important element in a web of factors and influences associated with such behavior and for some individuals it may promote or increase the power of these other factors."[52]

20.     Given the totality of the record before us, we agree with the view of the Surgeon General that: "a diverse body of research provides strong evidence that exposure to violence in the media can increase children's aggressive behavior in the short term." At the same time, we do recognize that "many questions remain regarding the short- and long-term effects of media violence, especially on violent

---

[46] Michael Males is a Senior Researcher for the Center on Juvenile and Criminal Justice and a Sociology Instructor at the University of California, Santa Cruz. He has written extensively on youth and social issues in the *New York Times* and academic journals.

[47] Males Comments at 9.

[48] *Id.* at 8-9.

[49] *Id.*

[50] *Id.*

[51] *Id.*

[52] Report to the Minister of Broadcasting of the Working Group: TV Violence Project, *Towards Precautionary Risk Management of TV Violence in New Zealand* at 19 (April 2004). The working group concluded in a related report that "despite occasional claims to the contrary and the proliferation of studies, the case that television can be regarded as a necessary and sufficient cause of societal violence remains unconfirmed." King, Bridgman, Smith, Bell, King, Harvey, Crothers, and Hassal, *Television Violence in New Zealand: A Study of Programming and Policy in International Context*, at Section A-1 (2003).

behavior."[53]  We note that a significant number of health professionals, parents and members of the general public are concerned about television violence and its effects on children.[54]

## III.    LAW AND POLICY ADDRESSING THE DISTRIBUTION OF VIOLENT TELEVISION PROGRAMMING

21.    Members of Congress asked the Commission to address the government's authority, consistent with the First Amendment, to restrict the broadcast or other distribution of excessively violent programming and what measures to constrain or regulate such programming are most likely to be sustained in court.[55]  Accordingly, we discuss below regulatory alternatives for protecting children from violent television content.  We begin, however, with a brief overview of the relevant constitutional framework.

22.    Violent speech and depictions of violence have been found by the courts to be protected by the First Amendment.[56]  However, "each medium of expression presents special First Amendment problems," with broadcasting historically receiving "the most limited First Amendment protection."[57]  Thus, even when broadcast speech "lies at the heart of First Amendment protection," the government may regulate it so long as its interest in doing so is "substantial" and the restriction is "narrowly tailored" to further that interest.[58]  While a restriction on the content of protected speech will generally be upheld only if it satisfies strict scrutiny, meaning that the restriction must further a compelling government interest and be the least restrictive means to further that interest, this exacting standard does not apply to the regulation of broadcast speech.

23.    In the realm of indecency, the U.S. Supreme Court has identified two principal reasons for the reduced First Amendment protection afforded to broadcasting:  first, its "uniquely pervasive presence in the lives of all Americans;" and second, its accessibility to children, coupled with the government's interests in the well-being of children and in supporting parental supervision of children.[59]  In light of these characteristics, the Court, in Pacifica,[60] upheld the Commission's authority to regulate the broadcast

---

[53] 2001 SG Report at Appendix 4-B (also noting that "[d]espite considerable advances in research, it is not yet possible to describe accurately how much exposure, of what types, for how long, at what ages, for what types of children, or in what types of settings will predict violent behavior in adolescents and adults").

[54] See, e.g., American Academy of Pediatrics, et. al, Joint Statement on the Impact of Entertainment Violence on Children, Congressional Public Health Summit (July 2000) (encouraging more study on the impact of violent entertainment on children and dialogue about what can be done to "enhance the health and well-being of America's children"); Parents, Media and Public Policy: A Kaiser Family Foundation Survey (Fall 2004) (a majority of parents say they are "very" concerned about the amount of violence that their children are exposed to on TV); SRBI/Time Magazine Poll (Mar. 18, 2005) (66% of people believe there is too much violence on television).

[55] See House Commerce Committee Letter at 1-2.

[56] Winters v. New York, 333 U.S. 507, 510 (1948) (magazines devoted to accounts of criminal deeds and stories and pictures of crime and bloodshed were "as much entitled to the protection of free speech as the best of literature."). But some have suggested that the current prohibitions on obscene and indecent speech could be lawfully applied to reach violence. See, e.g., Gloria Tristani, On Children and Television, Keynote Address at the Annenberg Public Policy Center's 5th Annual Conference on Children and Media (June 26, 2000), available at http://www.fcc.gov/Speeches/Tristani/2000/spgt009 html.

[57] FCC v. Pacifica Foundation, 438 U.S. 726, 744 (1978). See Action for Children's Television v. FCC, 58 F.3d 654, 660 (D.C. Cir. 1995) (en banc) ("ACT III").

[58] FCC v. League of Women Voters, 468 U.S. 364, 380-81 (1984); Prayze FM v. FCC, 214 F.3d 245, 252 (2d Cir. 2000).

[59] Pacifica, 438 U.S. at 748-50, citing Ginsberg v. New York, 390 U.S. 629 (1968).

[60] Pacifica, 438 U.S. at 748-50.

of indecent material. Relying on *Pacifica*, the U.S. Court of Appeals for the District of Columbia Circuit later concluded in *ACT III* that the "channeling" of indecent content to the hours between 10:00 p.m. and 6:00 a.m. would not unduly burden First Amendment rights.[61] It held that such regulation would promote the government's "compelling interest in supporting parental supervision of what children see and hear on the public airwaves." It also noted that it is "evident beyond the need for elaboration" that the government's "interest in safeguarding the physical and psychological well-being of a minor is compelling."[62] In addition, in light of relevant U.S. Supreme Court precedent, the D.C. Circuit refused in *ACT III* to insist on scientific evidence that indecent content harms children, concluding that the government's interest in the well-being of minors is not "limited to protecting them from clinically measurable injury."[63]

24.     *Time Channeling.* As stated above, members of Congress asked the Commission to address possible measures to protect children from excessively violent television content. We begin by discussing time channeling restrictions that would restrict such programming to hours when children are less likely to be in the viewing audience. We note that commenters disagreed about the constitutionality of such requirements. Pappas argued that they would be likely to pass constitutional muster because the government interests are substantially the same as those at stake in regulating broadcast indecency.[64] Other commenters maintain that such requirements would be unconstitutional and unworkable.[65]

25.     After carefully evaluating these comments and relevant precedent, we find that Congress could impose time channeling restrictions on excessively violent television programming in a constitutional manner. Just as the government has a compelling interest in protecting children from sexually explicit programming, a strong argument can be made, for the reasons discussed in Section II above, that the government also has a compelling interest in protecting children from violent programming and supporting parental supervision of minors' viewing of violent programming. We also believe that, if properly defined, excessively violent programming, like indecent programming, occupies a relatively low position in the hierarchy of First Amendment values because it is of "'slight social value as a step to truth.'"[66] Such programming is entitled to reduced First Amendment protection because of its pervasiveness and accessibility to children pursuant to the U.S. Supreme Court's reasoning in *Pacifica*.

26.     To be sure, the government, when imposing time channeling, would have to show that such regulation is a narrowly tailored means of vindicating its interests in promoting parental supervision and protecting children. In this regard, however, we note that while the alternative measures discussed below—viewer-initiated blocking and mandatory ratings—would impose lesser burdens on protected speech, we are skeptical that they will fully serve the government's interests in promoting parental supervision and protecting the well-being of minors.[67] In addition to these measures, as discussed below, another way of providing consumers greater control – and therefore greater ability to avoid violent programming – could be to require video channels to be offered on an "a la carte" basis.[68] As the D.C.

---

[61] *ACT III*, 58 F.3d at 656.

[62] *Id.* at 661.

[63] *Id. See id.* at 661-63, *citing Bethel School District No. 403 v. Fraser*, 478 U.S. 675, 684 (1986); *Pacifica*, 438 U.S. at 749-50; *Ginsberg v. New York*, 390 U.S. 629, 641-43 (1968).

[64] Pappas Comments at 8.

[65] *See* Center for Creative Voices in Media Comments at 9; Media Associations Comments at 58-59; Media Coalition Comments at 4.

[66] *Pacifica*, 438 U.S. at 746, *quoting Chaplinsky*, 315 U.S. at 572.

[67] *See ACT III*, 58 F.3d at 661 (citing evidence that parents are not in a position to exercise effective supervision over what their children see and hear on television and radio).

[68] *See infra* ¶¶ 48 *et seq.*

Circuit has noted in the context of indecency: "It is fanciful to believe that the vast majority of parents who wish to shield their children from indecent material can effectively do so without meaningful restrictions on the airing of broadcast indecency."[69] To cite just some of the relevant data, 81 percent of children ages two through seven sometimes watch television without adult supervision,[70] and 91 percent of children ages four through six have turned on the television by themselves.[71] In addition, as discussed below, the studies and surveys conducted to date tend to show that blocking technologies and the associated TV ratings system are of limited effectiveness in supporting parental supervision of minors' viewing habits.

27.     Generally, however, the sustainability of time channeling restrictions would depend on a number of specific evidentiary considerations. Therefore, should Congress wish to adopt time channeling restrictions, lawmakers should make specific findings to support such restrictions.[72] Significant issues that Congress may wish to address include the nature of the harm to children inflicted by violent television content, how to define such content,[73] and the ages of the children that the government is seeking to protect. For example, indecent material is channeled to the hours between 10:00 p.m. and 6:00 a.m. This "safe harbor" is based on evidence that children 17 years of age and under are less likely to be in the audience during these hours. With respect to violent program content, the research suggests that younger children are most at risk, possibly requiring a different conclusion as to the ages of children to be protected and the appropriate "safe harbor" hours.

28.     *Viewer-Initiated Blocking* and *Mandatory Ratings*. Besides time channeling, another possible means of protecting children from violent television content is to strengthen mechanisms that enable viewer-initiated blocking of such content. In 1996, Congress amended Title III of the Communications Act to require the incorporation of blocking technology into television sets.[74] As of January 1, 2000, all television sets manufactured in the United States or shipped in interstate commerce with a picture screen of thirteen inches or larger must be equipped with a "V-chip" system that can be programmed to block violent, sexual, or other programming that parents do not wish their children to view.[75] However, out of a total universe of 280 million sets in U.S. households,[76] only about 119 million sets in use today, or less than half, are equipped with V-chips.[77]

---

[69] *ACT III*, 58 F.3d at 663.

[70] U.S. Department of Education, *Strong Families, Strong Schools: Building Community Partnerships for Learning* (1994).

[71] *Kaiser Kids and Media Report* at 16.

[72] Although the government does not necessarily need evidence of clinically measurable injury to demonstrate a compelling interest in protecting children from harm, *see ACT III*, 58 F.3d at 660-63, legislative findings are likely to be important in defining the government interests at stake and in demonstrating use of narrowly tailored means. We note that courts have given Congress far more deference than the Commission with regard to the evidence necessary to sustain such restrictions. *See Turner I*, 512 U.S. at 666 ("Congress is not obligated, when enacting its statutes, to make a record of the type that an administrative agency or a court does to accommodate judicial review.").

[73] *See infra* Section IV.

[74] 47 U.S.C. § 303(x).

[75] *See Technical Requirements to Enable Blocking of Video Programming Based on Program Ratings*, 13 FCC Rcd 11248 (1998); 47 C.F.R. § 15.120(b).

[76] *See* Knowledge Networks SRI, *Home Technology Monitor Survey*, Spring 2004; Nielsen Media Research U.S. TV Household Estimates, 2003-04.

[77] *See* Broadcasting & Cable TVFAX, *TV Watch "Exposes" V-chip Critics* at 2 (July 8, 2005).

29. Based on the studies and surveys conducted to date, we believe that the evidence clearly points to one conclusion: the V-chip is of limited effectiveness in protecting children from violent television content. In order for V-chip technology to block a specific category of television programming, such as violent content, it must be activated. However, many parents do not even know if the television sets in their households incorporate this technology and, of those who do, many do not use it. In 2004, the Kaiser Family Foundation conducted a telephone survey of 1,001 parents of children ages 2-17.[78] The results showed: (1) only 15 percent of all parents have used the V-chip; (2) 26 percent of all parents have not bought a new television set since January 2000 (when the V-chip was first required in *all* sets); (3) 39 percent of parents have bought a new television set since January 2000, but do not think it includes a V-chip; and (4) 20 percent of parents know they have a V-chip, but have not used it.[79] According to a 2003 study, parents' low level of V-chip use is explained in part by parents' unawareness of the device and the "multi-step and often confusing process" necessary to use it.[80] Only 27 percent of parents in the study group could figure out how to program the V-Chip, and many parents "who might otherwise have used the V-Chip were frustrated by an inability to get it to work properly."[81] A March 2007 Zogby poll indicates, among other things, that 88 percent of respondents did not use a V-chip or cable box parental controls in the previous week, leading the Parents Television Council to call the television industry's V-chip education campaign "a failure."[82]

30. In addition to mandating inclusion of V-chip technology in television sets, the Act provides cable subscribers with some ways to block unwanted programming.[83] These provisions of the Act, however, do not benefit households receiving their television programming via over-the-air broadcasting or satellite. Further, similar to the V-chip, to take advantage of these measures a cable subscriber first must be aware of and then affirmatively request that such measures be employed. Finally, to receive these protections, a cable subscriber must take several steps and incur some costs.

31. Specifically, while cable operators provide their digital subscribers with advanced parental control technology,[84] those parental controls only are available to digital cable subscribers using digital cable set-top boxes.[85] Of the cable industry's 65,600,000 subscriber households, only 32,602,000 – less than half of all subscribers – subscribe to digital service.[86] Furthermore, while those digital cable households[87] likely have at least one cable operator-provided digital set-top box, many, if not most, of

---

[78] *See Parents, Media and Public Policy: A Kaiser Family Foundation Survey* (Fall 2004). The survey asked parents about their concerns regarding media content, their children's exposure to such content, and the appropriate measures to limit exposure to inappropriate content.

[79] *Id.* at 7.

[80] Annenberg Public Policy Center, *Parents' Use of the V-Chip to Supervise Children's Television Use* 3 (2003).

[81] *Id.* at 4.

[82] Parents Television Council, *PTC Declares the Industry's V-Chip Education Campaign a Failure* (March 15, 2007), available at www.parentstv.org/PTC/publications/release/2007/0305.asp.

[83] *See* 47 U.S.C. §§ 544(d)(2) & 560.

[84] *See, e.g.*, http://www.comcast.com/corporate/customers/parentalcontrols html ("Activated by a PIN number, you can set Parental Controls on your TV and/or cable set-top box to control the programs that can be viewed on your TV. There are three ways to block programs: By Channel[;] By Rating[;] [or] By Time Period.")

[85] Although cable operators provide some basic parental controls to analog cable subscribers, those parental controls (1) only are available to subscribers using certain analog set-top boxes, and (2) only allow subscribers to block entire channels. *See, e.g.*, http://www.controlyourtv.org/DetailPage.php?PageID=44.

[86] *See NCTA Statistics, available at* http://www.ncta.com/ContentView.aspx?contentId=54.

[87] A digital set-top box or a Digital Cable Ready television is required to receive digital cable service. *See Implementation of Section 304 of the Telecommunications Act of 1996: Commercial Availability of Navigation*

(continued....)

those homes do not have digital set-top boxes connected to every television used to view cable programming. Accordingly, the percentage of cable-connected television sets on which those advanced parental controls are available likely is even lower than the percentage of cable households that subscribe to digital cable services. Therefore, it does not appear that cable operator-provided advanced parental controls are available on a sufficient number of cable-connected television sets to be considered an effective solution at this time.

32.      We believe that further action to enable viewer-initiated blocking of violent television content would serve the government's interests in protecting the well-being of children and facilitating parental supervision and would be reasonably likely to be upheld as constitutional. As indicated above, however, reliance on blocking technology alone would probably not fulfill the government's interest in protecting the well-being of children. Blocking technology does not ensure that children are prevented from viewing violent programming unless it is activated, and courts have recognized the practical limits of parental supervision.[88]

33.      In addition, any successful viewer-initiated blocking regime with respect to violent programming would depend upon the adoption and successful implementation of an effective ratings system. Currently, to facilitate operation of the V-chip and other blocking mechanisms, broadcast, cable, and satellite television providers, on a voluntary basis, rate programming using the industry-devised TV ratings system guidelines and encode programs accordingly.[89] Most television programming, except for news and sports programming, carries an age-based TV rating set by program networks and producers, and most include content-based ratings as well.[90]

34.      Studies and surveys demonstrate, however, that the voluntary TV ratings system is of limited effectiveness in protecting children from violent television content. In the 2004 Kaiser survey discussed above, 50 percent of all parents surveyed stated that they have used the TV ratings. But about 4 in 10 parents (39 percent) stated that most programs are not rated accurately,[91] and many parents did not

---

(...continued from previous page)

*Devices*, 18 FCC Rcd 518 (2003). In order to receive encrypted digital cable programming on a Digital Cable Ready set, a CableCARD is required. *See id.* at 519. According to a report recently filed by NCTA in CS Docket No. 97-80, the 11 largest cable operators have deployed approximately 259,000 CableCARDs. See Letter from Neal M. Goldberg, Vice President and General Counsel, National Cable and Telecommunications Association, to Marlene H. Dortch, Secretary, Federal Communications Commission (filed March 26, 2007). Cable-provided parental controls are not available to subscribers using unidirectional Digital Cable Ready devices. *See, e.g.,* http://www.comcast.com/Customers/FAQ/FaqDetails.ashx?Id=2656; http://www.bendcable.com/cablecard.cfm.

[88] *See ACT III*, 58 F.3d at 661.

[89] *See* 47 U.S.C. § 303(w); *Video Programming Ratings*, 13 FCC Rcd 8232 (1998). In finding the voluntary ratings system consistent with the requirements of Sections 551(e)(1) and (2) of the Telecommunications Act of 1996, the Commission noted that the ratings system had been voluntarily proposed by a broad segment of the television industry and had been explicitly endorsed by nine prominent advocacy groups, including the American Medical Association, the American Academy of Pediatrics, American Psychological Association, Center for Media Education, Children's Defense Fund, Children Now, National Association of Elementary School Principals, National Education Association and the National PTA. Producers and distributors of uncut motion pictures have an alternative to the widely used television industry ratings system: they may use the Motion Picture Association of America's rating system (G, PG, PG-13, R and NC-17) in lieu of the TV ratings system.

[90] The age-based ratings are:  TV-Y (All Children); TV-Y7 (Directed to Older Children – age 7 and older); TV-G (General Audience); TV-PG (Parental Guidance Suggested); TV-14 (Parents Strongly Cautioned – may be unsuitable for children under 14); and TV-MA (Mature Audience Only – may be unsuitable for children under 17). The content-based descriptors are:  V (violence); FV (fantasy violence in children's programming); S (sexual content); D (suggestive dialogue); and L (strong language in programming).

[91] *Parents, Media and Public Policy:  A Kaiser Family Foundation Survey* (Fall 2004).

fully understand what the various ratings categories mean. For example, only 24 percent of parents of young children (two-six years old) could name any of the ratings that would apply to programming appropriate for children that age.[92] Only 12 percent of parents knew that the rating FV ("fantasy violence") is related to violent content, while 8 percent thought it meant "family viewing." One in five (20 percent) parents said that they had never heard of the TV ratings system, an increase from 14 percent in 2000 and 2001. A more recent survey indicates that only 8 percent of respondents could correctly identify the categories.[93]

      35. And, of course, ratings can only be effective in protecting children from inappropriate content if the parent understands the ratings information, and such information is accurate.[94] In a study published in the journal *Pediatrics*, parents concluded that half of television shows the industry had rated as appropriate for teenagers were in fact inappropriate, a finding the study authors called "a signal that the ratings are misleading."[95] Academics who have studied the television rating system share parents' assessment that the ratings are often inaccurate. A 2002 study found that many shows that should carry content descriptors do not, therefore leaving parents unaware of potentially objectionable material.[96] For example, the study found that 68 percent of prime-time network shows without an "L" descriptor contained "adult language," averaging nearly three scenes with such language per show.[97] In fact, "in all four areas of sensitive material – violence, sexual behavior, sexual dialogue, and adult language – the large majority of programs that contain such depictions are not identified by a content descriptor."[98] The study's authors concluded that "[p]arents who might rely solely on the content-based categories to block their children's exposure to objectionable portrayals would be making a serious miscalculation, as the content descriptors actually identify only a small minority of the full range of violence, sex, and adult language found on television."[99] A 2004 study also raised serious questions about the accuracy of television ratings. It found that there was more coarse language broadcast during TV-PG programs than those rated TV-14, just the opposite of what these age-based ratings would lead a viewer to believe.[100]

---

[92] *Id.* at 6. While 28 percent of parents of young children knew what the TV-Y7 rating means (programming directed to children age 7 and older), 13 percent thought it meant the opposite (programming directed to children under 7) and the rest did not know (38 percent) or had not ever heard of the ratings system at all (21 percent).

[93] Parents Television Council, *PTC Declares the Industry's V-Chip Education Campaign a Failure* (March 15, 2007), available at www.parentstv.org/PTC/publications/release/2007/0305.asp.

[94] *See Marketing Violent Entertainment to Children: A Fifth Follow-up Review of Industry Practices in the Motion Picture, Music Recording & Electronic Game Industries, Federal Trade Commission,* ("*FTC Report*") at 33, *available at* http://www.ftc.gov/reports/violence/070412MarketingViolentEChildren.pdf (rel. Apr. 12. 2007) (stating the "[p]arents should be able to rely on complete rating systems where decisions are made after a fair review of all appropriate content, and where rating and labeling information reasonably informs them about the content").

[95] David A. Walsh & Douglas A. Gentile, *A Validity Test of Movie, Television, and Video-Game Ratings,* 107 Pediatrics 1302, 1306 (2001).

[96] *See* Dale Kunkel, *et al., Deciphering the V-Chip: An Examination of the Television Industry's Program Rating Judgments,* 52 Journal of Communications 112 (2002).

[97] *See id.* at 132; *see also id.* at 131 (finding that 20 percent of shows rated TV-G – supposedly appropriate for all ages – included objectionable language, including "bastard," "bitch," "shit," and "whore").

[98] *Id.* at 136.

[99] *Id.*

[100] Barbara K. Kaye & Barry S. Sapolsky, *Offensive Language in Prime-Time Television: Four Years After Television Age and Content Ratings,* 48 Journal of Broadcasting & Electronic Media 554, 563-64 (2004); *see also Effectiveness of Media Rating Systems: Subcommittee of Science, Technology, and Space of the Senate Comm. On Commerce, Science & Transp.,* 107th Congress (2004) (statement of Ms. Patti Miller, director, Children and the Media Program for Children Now) ("Can parents depend on the accuracy of the ratings systems? Sadly, the answer is no.").

The Parents Television Council ("PTC") and the Annenberg Public Policy Center also have conducted studies indicating that the voluntary TV ratings system is inaccurate, inconsistently applied, and cannot fully address parental concerns over children's TV viewing.[101]

36.     An economist studying the question of why networks consistently "underlabel" their programs concluded that they are likely responding to economic incentives.[102]  He found that programs with more restrictive ratings command lower advertising revenues.[103]  The desire to charge more for commercials and fear of "advertiser backlash" over shows with more restrictive ratings "means that networks have incentives to resist the provision of content-based information."[104]

37.     To address these issues, Congress could seek to establish a mandatory ratings system that would address the shortcomings of the current system set forth above.  Such a system could be defended on the grounds that it merely requires the disclosure of truthful information about a potentially harmful product (violent television programming), thereby advancing the compelling government interests without significantly burdening First Amendment rights.  It could also be defended as a necessary predicate for the operation of a successful system of viewer-initiated blocking.  As stated above, however, although mandatory television ratings would impose lesser burdens on protected speech, we believe the evidence demonstrates that they would not fully serve the government's interest in the well-being of minors given the limits of parental supervision recognized by the D.C. Circuit in *ACT III*.[105]  Experience also leads us to question whether such a ratings system would ever be sufficiently accurate given the myriad of practical difficulties that would accompany any comprehensive effort to ensure the accuracy of ratings.  Moreover, such a requirement may have an unintended practical consequence.  There is some evidence that TV ratings may actually serve to attract certain underage viewers to programming that is violent or is otherwise labeled as not intended for a child audience.[106]

---

[101] Parents Television Council, *The Ratings Sham: TV Executives Hiding Behind A System That Doesn't Work* (April 2005).  Annenberg Public Policy Center, *Parents' Use of the V-chip to Supervise Children's Television Use* (Feb. 2003), at 4.  PTC examined prime time entertainment programs from the first two weeks of the November 2003, February 2004, and May 2004 sweeps on the seven commercial broadcast networks that existed at that time.  The study period comprised 638 shows (totaling 528 hours).  According to PTC, each of the networks studied inaccurately and inconsistently applied the TV ratings content descriptors to the programs under consideration.  For example, 81 percent of CBS's TV-14-rated shows containing sexual dialogue lacked the D descriptor (suggestive dialogue) and 82 percent of the WB's TV-14-rated shows containing sexual behavior lacked the S descriptor (sexual content).  PTC ascribed this lack of accuracy to the fact that the networks rate their own programs.  Several mothers that participated in the Annenberg study stated that because there are multiple televisions in their homes (the average family had four television sets), a child motivated to watch a blocked program can find it on a non-V-chip television.  In addition, several of the study participants complained that the V-chip did not block content about which they were concerned – specifically commercials, promotions for upcoming television programs, and news programs.  Finally, several expressed dissatisfaction with the confusing nature of the TV ratings.

[102] *See* James T. Hamilton, *Who Will Rate the Ratings?* in *The V-Chip Debate: Content Filtering from Television to the Internet* 133, 143, 149 (Monroe E. Price, ed. 1998); *see also FTC Report* at 3  (reporting that some critics of the MPAA movie ratings system allege "ratings creep" and that "[i]t has been argued that studios have a financial incentive to obtain a PG-13 rating, a rating that does not restrict admission to anyone but tolerates a substantial amount of violent content attractive to 12- to 17-year-olds").

[103] *See id.* at 143.

[104] *Id.* at 149; *see also* Kunkel, 52 Journal of Communications at 114 ("[T]he prospect that applying 'higher' ratings to a program could reduce audience size raises a self-interest concern regarding the accuracy with which judgments about program ratings are determined.").

[105] *See ACT III*, 58 F.3d at 661.

[106] *See* University of California, Santa Barbara *et. al.*, *National Television Violence Study: Scientific Papers*, 1994-1995, III-45 ("The well known admonition 'parental discretion advised' had a strong and positive effect on boys'

(continued....)

## IV. DEFINING VIOLENT OR EXCESSIVELY OR GRATUITOUSLY VIOLENT PROGRAMMING

38.     Members of Congress asked the Commission to address whether it would be in the public interest to adopt a definition of "excessively violent programming harmful to children"[107] and to consider the constitutional limitations on the government's ability to formulate and implement such a definition.[108] While developing a definition would be challenging, we believe that Congress could do so.

39.     Several considerations are relevant to the adoption of a definition, including the regulatory function of the definition.  A definition used for TV ratings purposes might be based on different criteria than a definition used for identifying video programming that must not be shown or must be channeled to a later hour.  For example, the definition used in a mandatory ratings regime intended to facilitate parental control might take into account a depiction's potential for harm without requiring a finding of a likelihood of harm.  Ratings and blocking regulations might require multiple definitions for different kinds of violent programming to which parents might want to restrict their children's access.  Another variable is what type and degree of violent content the research demonstrates, with a reasonable probability, is harmful to children.

40.     In addition, any definition would have to be sufficiently clear to provide fair notice to regulated entities.[109]  NAB and other commenters principally argue that violent programming cannot be sufficiently defined to give affected parties the requisite notice to be able to predictably comply with any such regulation.[110]  Moreover, to the extent regulations based on content are constitutionally permissible, the context of the speech may have to be factored into the balance.  For example, speech that might otherwise be unprotected as obscene receives protection if it has serious literary, artistic, political or scientific value.[111]  In contrast, in certain settings the government has greater ability to control indecent speech to the extent such speech is of "such slight social value as a step to truth that any benefit that may

---

(...continued from previous page)
interest in viewing reality-action programs, and the effect was strongest for boys in the older group. . . .  Older boys were especially interested in the target movie when it was rated 'PG-13' or 'R' and completely avoided it when it was rated 'G.'").  *See also FTC Report* at 4-5 (indicating that movie marketing targeted toward older teens may also attract younger teens).

[107] *See House Commerce Committee Letter* at 1.

[108] *Id.*

[109] A number of definitional attempts in the past have been unable to overcome this hurdle.  For example, attempts to regulate "excess violence" defined as "the depiction of acts of violence in such a graphic and/or bloody manner as to exceed common limits of custom and candor, or in such a manner that it is apparent that the predominant appeal of the material is portrayal of violence for violence's sake" have been held "void for vagueness."  A U.S. District Court found that the definition of the term makes the decision of what constitutes "excess violence" an entirely subjective one giving little, if any, objective guidance to those required to comply or to officials charged with enforcement. *See Allied Artists Pictures Corp. v. Alford*, 410 F. Supp. 1348 (W.D. Tenn. 1976) (striking down a local ordinance containing the term "excess violence" under void for vagueness doctrine in the context of the use of obscene language found in motion pictures); *see also Video Software Dealers Ass'n v. Webster*, 773 F. Supp. 1275, 1280 (W.D. Mo. 1991), *aff'd* 968 F.2d 684 (8th Cir. 1992) (finding unconstitutional a statute that included violent material within the definition of obscenity).

[110] NAB Comments at 43;  NCTA Comments at 3; Media Associations Comments at 44; Media Institute Comments at 2 (maintaining that establishing a definition that can capture the nuanced depictions of violence seen in dramas, comedies, and educational features, while allowing for predictability in enforcement, would be a difficult task).

[111] *See Miller*, 413 U.S. at 24.

be derived from them is clearly outweighed by the social interest in order and morality."[112]  In the indecency context, the D.C. Circuit addressed the "merit" issue as follows: "[S]ince the overall value of the work will not necessarily alter the impact of certain words or phrases on children, the FCC's approach is permissible under controlling case law; merit is properly treated as a factor in determining whether material is patently offensive, but it does not render such material per se not indecent."[113]

41.     Judicial decisions and scholarly articles discussing violence almost invariably make this definitional point by referencing classic works of literature of undisputed merit that involve graphic violence.  For example, in a case involving violent video games, Judge Posner opined that even the sponsors of the regulation would no doubt concede that restrictions would not be warranted:

> if the question were whether to forbid children to read without the
> presence of an adult the Odyssey, with its graphic descriptions of
> Odysseus's grinding out the eye of Polyphemus with a heated, sharpened
> stake, killing the suitors, and hanging the treacherous maidservants; or
> The Divine Comedy with its graphic descriptions of the tortures of the
> damned; or War and Peace with its graphic descriptions of execution by
> firing squad, death in childbirth, and death from war wounds.[114]

The UCLA Center for Communications Policy notes in its *1997 TV Violence Report*:

> For centuries, violence has been an important element of storytelling, and
> violent themes have been found in the Bible, The Iliad and The Odyssey,
> fairy tales, theater, literature, film and, of course, television.
> Descriptions of violence in the Bible have been important for teaching
> lessons and establishing a moral code.  Lessons of the evils of jealousy
> and revenge are learned from the story of Cain and Abel.  Early fairy
> tales were filled with violence and gruesomeness designed to frighten
> children into behaving and to teach them right from wrong.[115]

42.     Several commenters advocate adopting specific definitions.  Those that do chose pre-existing definitions in the literature or selected regulatory proxies as a model.  For example, Pappas Telecasting suggests that the Commission essentially adopt the definition used by the *National TV Violence Study*, which defined violence as "any overt depiction of a credible threat of physical force or the actual use of such force intended to physically harm an animate being or group of beings."[116] Morality in Media ("MIM") suggests enhancing the existing indecency definition by including references to violence.[117]  According to MIM, indecent speech should be defined as content that, in context, describes

---

[112]  *Pacifica*, 438 U.S. at 746 (Stevens, J., Rehnquist, J., and Burger, C.J., plurality) (citing *Chaplinksy*, 315 U.S. at 572).

[113]  *Action for Children's Television v. FCC*, 852 F.2d 1332, 1340 (D.C. Cir. 1988) ("*ACT I*").

[114]  *See American Amusement Machine Association v. Kendrick*, 244 F.3d 572, 576.

[115]  *See 1997 UCLA Television Violence Monitoring Report* at 8, *available at* http://ccp.ucla.edu.Webreport96.thestudy htm ("1997 UCLA Report"); *see also* Schecter, *Savage Pastimes—A Cultural History of Violent Entertainment*, St. Martin's Press (2005) (citing the same).

[116]  Pappas Comments at 5-6, citing *Third National TV Violence Study* at § II.D.1.  Although the *National Television Violence Study* used this definition, it did not include news, sports, or religious programming within its survey because of contractual restrictions imposed by its sponsors.

[117]  MIM Comments at 3.  MIM states that depictions of simulated war activities, especially those purporting to be distant in time, would not meet the "outrageously offensive or outrageously disgusting" test.  MIM states, however, that there are warlike activities that the average person would consider outrageously offensive or outrageously

(continued....)

or depicts: "(1) sexual or excretory activities or organs or (2) outrageously offensive or outrageously disgusting violence or (3) severed or mutilated human bodies or body parts, in terms patently offensive as measured by contemporary community standards for the broadcast medium." MIM defines violence as: "intense, rough or injurious use of physical force or treatment either recklessly or with an apparent intent to harm."[118]

43.     The Media Institute maintains that establishing a definition that can capture the nuanced depictions of violence seen in dramas, comedies, and educational features, while allowing for predictability in enforcement, would be a difficult task.[119] It urges the Commission to consider the context of physical force seen in a football game, a "Road Runner" cartoon, the Holocaust drama *Schindler's List*, a *The Three Stooges* short, an airing of the evening news with discussion of violent crime, and a science fiction film such as *Star Wars*. It argues that instances of violence, essential to each of these protected forms of speech, serve a completely different function in each instance based on context. It argues that, under MIM's proposal, the media could not with any surety report the news, broadcast dramatic works appropriate for adults, or even air professional sporting events.[120] NAB asserts that, if the definition of violence from the *National Television Violence Study* were used to regulate television programming, many of the most popular shows in television history, such as *Hill Street Blues*, *Gunsmoke*, and *The Untouchables*, would have been subject to some type of government restriction.[121] NAB and other commenters argue that the Commission cannot sufficiently define violent programming to give affected parties the requisite notice to be able to predictably comply with any such regulation.

44. We believe that developing an appropriate definition of excessively violent programming would be possible, but such language needs to be narrowly tailored and in conformance with judicial precedent.[122] Any definition would need to be clear enough to provide fair warning of the conduct required. A definition sufficient to give notice of upcoming violent programming content to parents and potential viewers could make use of, or be a refinement of, existing voluntary rating system definitions or could make use of definitions used in the research community when studying the consequences of violent programming. For more restrictive time channeling rules, a definition based on the scientific literature discussed above, which recognizes the factors most important to determining the likely impact of violence on the child audience, could be developed.[123] For example, such a definition might cover depictions of physical force against an animate being that, in context, are patently offensive. In determining whether such depictions are patently offensive, the Government could consider among other factors the presence

---

(...continued from previous page)
disgusting, such as a close-up depiction of a scalping, a beheading, or a mutilation. Other combative activities, such as a cowboy "shoot-out" or a laser gun battle in *Star Wars* would not get the same reaction of outrageousness or disgust. *Id.* at 3-4.

[118] *Id.*

[119] Media Institute Comments at 2. The Media Institute is a non-profit research foundation specializing in communications policy and First Amendment issues.

[120] *Id.* at 8.

[121] NAB Reply Comments at 6-7. NAB notes that the impossibility of defining violence in a precise, rational, and non-arbitrary manner is shown by the results of a survey of television violence conducted at Concordia College. This survey reportedly found 19 acts of violence in *The Little Mermaid*, an animated children's film, but only 12 acts of violence in Alfred Hitchcock's *North by Northwest* and 21 acts of violence in a documentary about the Civil War. NAB questions whether *North by Northwest* is really less violent and more suitable for young children than *The Little Mermaid*.

[122] We note that the courts have rejected arguments that the definition of indecency is unconstitutionally vague and overbroad. *See ACT I*, 852 F.2d at 1340.

[123] *See supra* note 34 (discussing the factors described by researcher Barbara Wilson).

of weapons, whether the violence is extensive or graphic, and whether the violence is realistic.[124]

## V.    CONCLUSIONS AND RECOMMENDATIONS

45.     In response to the specific questions posed, we draw the following conclusions.  First, with respect to the evidence of harm to children from viewing violent television content, there is strong evidence that exposure to violence in the media can increase aggressive behavior in children, at least in the short term.

46.     Second, although there are constitutional barriers to directly limiting or time channeling the distribution of violent television programming, the Supreme Court's *Pacifica* decision and other decisions relating to restrictions on the broadcast of indecent content provide possible parallels for regulating violent television content.  Third, while there are legal, evidentiary, analytical, and social science obstacles that need to be overcome in defining harmful violence, Congress likely has the ability and authority to craft a sustainable definition.

47.     Finally, we note that the 109th Congress was considering an extensive bill, introduced by Senators Rockefeller and Hutchinson, designed to protect children from excessive violence on television.[125]  The bill also proposed that the Commission consider and report on the effectiveness of the current technology and of consumer understanding of the technology and ratings system.[126]  This *Report*, in essence, serves the purpose contemplated in the bill.  Our analysis above indicates that the current technology "fix," including but not limited to consumer understanding of the technology and voluntary ratings system, is not effective in protecting children from violent programming.  Given the findings in this *Report*, we believe action should be taken to address violent programming.  Industry could on its own initiative commit itself to reducing the amount of excessively violent programming viewed by children.  Broadcasters could adopt a family hour at the beginning of prime time, during which they decline to air violent content.[127]  Multichannel video programming providers (MVPDs) could provide consumers greater choice in how they purchase their programming so that they could avoid violent programming.  Under such an approach, consumers could select the channels they want to pay for, and opt out of those that they do not.  In short, an a la carte regime would enable viewers to buy their television channels individually or in smaller bundles.  In this manner, consumers could avoid purchasing those channels that tend to air more violent programming.  Cable and DBS operators could implement a la carte in a variety of ways.  For example, it could be limited to digital cable customers who would be permitted to "opt out" of cable programming, requesting not to receive certain cable channels and having their package price reduced accordingly ("channel blocking and reimbursement").

48.     Alternatively, customers could be allowed to "opt in" to particular cable programs.  This is how premium channels are offered today.  In Hong Kong, for example, consumers can select and pay for only the channels they want.  A family that wants to watch sports, movies, news and children's programming can receive 15 free channels plus a selection of 11 additional digital channels including ESPN, HBO, CNN Headline News, National Geographic, Animal Planet, and Discovery for $27.50 per

---

[124] *See id. (citing* Wilson, Smith, Potter, Kunkel, Linz, Colvin, and Donnerstein, *Violence in Children's Television Programming:  Assessing the Risks*, Journal of Communications (Mar. 2003)).  *See also Standards for the Depiction of Violence*, Issued By ABC, CBS, and NBC (December 1992) (suggesting factors relevant to whether portrayals of violence are gratuitous or excessive).

[125] Indecent and Gratuitous and Excessively Violent Programming Control Act of 2005, S. 616, 109th Cong. (2005).

[126] *Id.* at § 4.

[127] *See, e.g., FTC Report* at i, 4, 20-21 (discussing industry advertising initiatives, including the MPAA initiative not to advertise R-rated movies in media with an under-17 audience of more than 35 percent, but also noting that the industry continues to advertise unrated DVDs and R-rates movies on television shows popular with children under age 17, and that some advertising violated the MPAA standards).

month. To get the same channels in Washington, DC, it would cost $82.00 per month.[128] Another option would be to allow consumers to choose a specific number of channels from a menu of available programming for a fixed price – e.g., 10 channels for $20, 20 channels for $30, etc. Customers then would be able to receive – and pay for – only that programming that they are comfortable bringing into their homes. For example, in Canada, digital subscribers can buy channels individually or enjoy significant savings on a "5 pack," a "10 pack" or a "15 pack" of their own choosing.

49. In sum, Congress could implement a time channeling solution, as discussed above, and/or mandate some other form of consumer choice in obtaining video programming, such as the provision by MVPDs of video channels provided on family tiers or on an a la carte basis (e.g., channel blocking and reimbursement).

## VI. ORDERING CLAUSES

50. Accordingly, **IT IS ORDERED** that, pursuant to the authority contained in sections 4(i), 303(g), 303(r), and 403 of the Communications Act, 47 U.S.C. §§ 154(i), 303, and 403, this Report **IS ADOPTED**.

51. It is **FURTHER ORDERED** that the Office of Legislative Affairs shall deliver copies of this *Report* to the appropriate committees and subcommittees of the United States House of Representatives and the United States Senate.

52. It is **FURTHER ORDERED** that the proceeding in MB Docket No. 04-261 **IS TERMINATED**.

FEDERAL COMMUNICATIONS COMMISSION

Marlene H. Dortch
Secretary

---

[128] As a result of competition and choice, consumers in Hong Kong are paying less on their cable bills. From 1995 to 2002, Hong Kong's cable bills increased 13%. Then a new video competitor came on the scene with an a la carte option it called "true consumer choice." Since that time, the monthly bills for Hong Kong cable customers have fallen by 9%. In the United States, by contrast, cable prices have increased almost 20% since 2002 and more then 90% since 1995.

# APPENDIX

## Commenters filing in MB Docket No. 04-261*

American Civil Liberties Union ("ACLU")
Center for Creative Voices in Media/Caucus for Television Producers/Peggy Charren ("CCVM")
Children's Media Policy Coalition ("CMPC"):
      Action Coalition for Media Education
      American Academy of Child and Adolescent Psychiatry
      American Academy of Pediatrics
      American Psychological Association
      Benton Foundation
      Children Now
      National Institute on Media and the Family
      National PTA
      Office of Communication of the United Church of Christ
Coalition for Independent Ratings Services ("CIRS"):
      Coalition for Quality Children's Media
      Critics, Inc.
      Family Style Film Guide
      Grading the Movies
      PSV Ratings, Inc.
Corporation for Public Broadcasting/Association of Public Television Stations ("CPB"/"APTS")
Craig A. Anderson, Ph.D., Iowa State University
Joanne Cantor, Ph.D., University of Wisconsin-Madison
Jerry Kroth, Ph.D., Santa Clara University
Media Coalition ("MC"):
      American Booksellers Foundation for Free Expression
      Association of American Publishers
      Comic Book Legal Defense Fund
      Freedom to Read Foundation
      Entertainment Software Association
      Interactive Entertainment Merchants Association
      Magazine Publishers of America
      Motion Picture Association of America
      National Association of Record Merchandisers
      Publishers Marketing Association
      Recording Industry Association of America
      Video Software Dealers Association
Media Associations ("MAS"):
      American Advertising Federation
      American Association of Advertising Agencies
      Association of National Advertisers, Inc.
      Motion Picture Association of America
      National Association of Broadcasters
      Satellite Broadcasting and Communications Association
Media Institute ("MI")
Michael Males, University of California, Santa Cruz
Morality in Media ("MIM")
Nancy Signorielli, Ph.D, University of Delaware
National Association of Broadcasters ("NAB")
National Cable and Telecommunications Association ("NCTA")

National Hockey League ("NHL")
Pappas Telecasting Companies ("Pappas")
Satellite Broadcasting and Communications Association ("SBCA")
Sesame Workshop
Tim Collings (V-chip inventor)

## Reply Comments

Capitol Broadcasting
Children's Media Policy Coalition
Community Broadcasters Association
Consumer Electronics Association
National Association of Broadcasters


*The Commission has also received hundreds of comments from concerned individuals in this proceeding. These comments are available through the Commission's electronic comment filing system.

## STATEMENT OF
## CHAIRMAN KEVIN J. MARTIN

**Re: *In the Matter of Violent Television Programming and Its Impact On Children*, MB Docket No. 04-261**

For decades, parents, healthcare professionals, and government officials have discussed and debated the impact of excessively violent programming on children. In fact almost 70% of respondents in a poll conducted for the Associated Press said there was too much violence on television. Four years ago, members of Congress asked the Commission to conduct an inquiry and to issue a report examining the harmful impact of violent video programming on children and what if anything Congress could do about it.

The concern about the potential impact of excessively violent programming is not surprising given that in the Children's Television Act, Congress noted that by the time the average child is eighteen years old, he or she will have watched between 10,000 and 15,000 hours of television. As stated in our Report, children on average watch between two and four hours of TV per day. Even the youngest children – those age six and under – watch an average of two hours of television each day, according to the Kaiser Family Foundation.

To assess the impact of violent programming on children, the Commission reviewed numerous studies conducted by the medical and social science communities. Research on whether watching violent programming actually causes aggressive behavior in children is inconclusive. However, major studies, including those by the Surgeon General and the Federal Trade Commission, have found that exposure to violent content on TV is associated with an increase in aggressive or violent behavior in children. In addition, a joint statement by major medical associations including the American Academy of Pediatrics, the American Medical Association and the American Psychiatric Association identified some of the effects of exposure to violence as being emotional desensitization towards violence in real life and having a higher tendency for violent behavior later in life. In other words, the evidence does not prove causation, but it does demonstrate a strong correlation.

These findings make clear, and the Commission today affirms, that exposure to violent programming can be harmful to children.

When it comes to protecting their children from such harm, parents are the first and last line of defense. Thus, it is critical then that they have the necessary tools to protect their children. Today the Commission concludes that current blocking technologies and ratings systems are insufficient and do not fully serve the interest of promoting parental supervision and protecting children. Less than half of the TV sets in American households are capable of blocking content that is not suitable for children. Even parents who have TVs equipped with a V-chip need more help. According to a recent Zogby poll, 88% of parents did not use a V-chip or a cable blocking device. In part, blocking solutions don't work because they are dependent on an imperfect television ratings system. Only 8% of respondents in the Zogby poll could correctly identify the ratings categories.

Clearly, steps should be taken to protect children from excessively violent programming. Some might say such action is long overdue. Parents need more tools to protect children from excessively violent programming. And, as the Commission finds today, they need tools that address the violent programming on all platforms—broadcast, cable and satellite.

I have long encouraged industry to give parents more direct control over the television content that comes into their homes. Broadcasters could reinstate the Family Hour at the beginning of prime-time, during which they would air only programs appropriate for children. Cable and satellite operators could enable parents to avoid purchasing channels that tend to show excessively violent programming by allowing them to purchase channels individually or in smaller bundles as they currently do for "premium channels" like HBO.

Whenever government considers such regulations, it must do so with great care and deliberation. For example, real life violence shown in a news story is not the same as fictional violence graphically depicted for purposes of "entertainment". Congress specifically asked the Commission to consider whether it would be possible to restrict the showing of violent programming during the hours of the day when children are likely to be watching television. The United States Supreme Court has upheld this sort of time channeling in the context of indecent programming. In that context, the Supreme Court ruled that the government could apply regulations when the government's interest was "substantial" and the restriction was "narrowly tailored." The Supreme Court emphasized two factors: the "pervasive presence in the lives of all Americans," and the government's interests in the well-being of children and in supporting parental supervision of children.

The television industry has already developed definitions of violence that is used in their ratings system. Specifically, the TV Parental Guidelines developed by the television industry include ratings that indicate the presence of "fantasy violence," "no violence," "moderate violence," "intense violence," and "graphic violence." Thus, it appears that the industry agrees with some basic definition of violence in programming, at least for use with blocking technologies. I therefore question commenters' arguments that violence can be defined sufficiently for ratings and blocking purposes, but not defined sufficiently for purposes of time channeling requirements.

Requiring cable and satellite television providers to offer programming in a more a la carte manner would be a more content neutral means for Congress to regulate violent programming and therefore would raise fewer constitutional issues. All of the versions of a la carte would keep government out of regulating content directly while enabling consumers, including parents, to receive the programming they want and believe to be appropriate for their families. For instance, cable operators already block any channel that a consumer requests to be blocked. One form of a la carte could simply require the cable operator to reimburse consumers for the channels they request to have blocked. While the Constitution protects the right to speak, it certainly doesn't protect a right to get *paid* for that speech. Cable operators also could offer to block and reimburse only those channels not subject to time channeling restrictions.

Multichannel video distributors in other countries already sell cable channels in a more a la carte fashion. For instance, In Hong Kong, consumers can select and pay for only the channels they want. A family who wants to watch sports, movies, news and children's programming can receive 15 free channels plus a selection of 11 additional digital channels including ESPN, HBO, CNN Headline News, National Geographic, Animal Planet, and Discovery for only $27.50 per month. To get the same channels in Washington, DC, it would cost $82.00 per month.

Similarly, in Canada, after buying basic cable, digital subscribers can buy channels individually or enjoy significant savings on a "5 pack", a "10 pack", or a "15 pack" of their own choosing.

It has long been my hope that the broadcast, cable and satellite industries would address content issues on their own, providing parents with effective tools to protect their children. Today the Commission, in response to specific Congressional questions, concludes that exposure to violent programming can be harmful to children and that Congress could provide parents more tools to limit their children's exposure to violent programming in a Constitutional way.

## STATEMENT OF
## COMMISSIONER MICHAEL J. COPPS

**Re:**      *In the Matter of Violent Television Programming and Its Impact on Children,*
        **MB Docket No. 04-261**

As I travel across the country talking with people about our nation's media, I consistently hear from parents about what their children are seeing on television. I hear many voices but one common refrain – parents are afraid of many of the images television sends, upset at the kinds of behavior certain programming seems to condone, and totally turned off by the extraordinary and escalating violence being broadcast into our living rooms.

Television is perhaps the most powerful force at work in the world today. When used for good, it can enlighten minds, convey powerful ideas, educate, and lay the foundation for human development. But when it is used to mislead, misrepresent and distort, it can – it does – inflict lasting harm. Most of the evidence amassed over the past half century indicates a relationship between gratuitous violence and harmful effects – personal, psychological and social. While research continues on how children are affected by what they watch, it seems close to indisputable that there are indeed unfortunate and negative outgrowths from the spreading virus of broadcast violence.

Congress requested the FCC to report on the issue and to develop some options for legislators to consider. This violence report is the Commission's response to that request. It surveys the problem, presents our considered "take" on the issue and develops several options for Congress to consider should it decide to develop legislation on the matter. It tees up such options as time channeling, viewer initiated blocking and mandatory ratings, as well as a la carte or bundling approaches in the cable and DBS context. Congress retains, of course, the prerogative to act, just as the judiciary has the prerogative of responding to legislation that is challenged in the courts. The instant report marries no one approach but instead responds to the request for analysis and options.

The facts are extraordinary and alarming. Children watch on average between two and four hours of television every day; young children are masters of the remote control; and they often watch television unsupervised. The research taken as a whole strongly suggests that children's constant exposure to violence on television can be desensitizing, damaging and even devastating to them and to society-at-large.

We all have important roles to play to protect our children from violent programming – parents, industry, the FCC, and Congress. Parents are of course the first line of defense, and without their active involvement it is difficult to envision a successful cure for the violence virus. Yet significant evidence indicates that no tools thus far available have been successful in containing the epidemic. This would include the V-chip, other control technologies and the existing television program ratings system. Industry's efforts have obviously not solved the problem and the preoccupation of some media – especially large national conglomerates often more interested in selling products to young people than in removing violence from the airwaves – does not provide much confidence that it will move to solve the problem. Given the impact of gratuitous violence on children and the pervasiveness of this kind of programming in our homes, it becomes altogether appropriate for Congress and the Commission to address the issue.

I am pleased that the Commission unanimously concludes in today's report that it is appropriate for Congress to entertain action against program violence. Congress has the opportunity, should it choose to do so, to establish innovative, meaningful, and constitutional ways for safeguarding our children from violent programming when they are most likely to be in the viewing audience. As this issue continues to gather momentum, I hope we can have a dialogue across the nation on the challenges that will attend the various options we tee up today and others that Congress and others will no doubt suggest. This is the beginning, not the end, of the debate. I for one proceed acutely sensitive to the need for a carefully crafted approach. I want to see a solution that solves the problem without creating others. I recognize that it is not an easy challenge to develop rules that pass constitutional muster, but given what amounts to a public health crisis at hand, I believe it is a challenge that must be met. Serious and festering problems require solutions, so that the question here is not *whether* we should address the issue, but *how* we should address it. Working together – citizens, industry and government – there is simply no reason why we should not be able to find workable solutions.

Finally, I commend the Chairman and all my colleagues for supporting this report and for their helpful suggestions to make it better. I hope our action today will be an important first step in safeguarding our children from excessively violent television programming.

**STATEMENT OF
COMMISSIONER JONATHAN S. ADELSTEIN
APPROVING IN PART & CONCURRING IN PART**

*Re*: **Violent Television Programming and Its Impact on Children,** *Report,* **MB Docket No. 04-261**

America is hooked on violence. That manifests itself in news coverage with the credo, "if it bleeds, it leads." To an alarming extent, the same credo applies to much entertainment programming and even some commercials. The top ten highest rated broadcast programs consistently have programs with violent content leading the pack.[1] In the primetime ratings game, violence sells and our children are innocent bystanders. This very unfortunate state of affairs is the shared responsibility of networks, broadcasters, cable operators and programmers, advertisers, and ultimately viewers.

There is considerable evidence in the social science literature that violence in the media can cause children to act more violently or aggressively. Particularly in light of the spasm of unconscionable violence at Virginia Tech, but just as importantly in light of the excessive violent crime that daily afflicts our nation, there is a basis for appropriate federal action to curb violence in the media.

This is an issue of deep personal significance to me as a parent of small children. I am particularly fortunate that my career choice has sensitized me to the relentless assault of violent content on television that confronts me and my children. A turning point for me came at my first confirmation hearing for this position, when Senator Sam Brownback showed me a study about how the brain scans changed for people while they were watching violent programming. Ever since, I have viewed, particularly over my children's shoulders in those instances when I let them watch, the cavalcade of violence that afflicts children's and adult programming alike.

It is clear that parents are the first, last *and* best line of defense against all forms of objectionable content. Speaking as a parent, the problem is that in today's media landscape, families have to navigate through a sea of violence. Making a bad situation worse, most parents don't know about the navigational tools available to them, so they are like 17th Century sailors subject to the whims of an angry sea when they could be using more modern techniques. The following chart, which simply reflects the casual observations of me and my staff, is meant to illustrate the volume of violent shows on television during the current primetime line-up.

---

[1] *See* Nielsen Media Research ratings for week of March 19 through 25, 2007, which reveal that six of the top ten broadcast shows among all households and five of the top show among adults 18-49 contained graphic violent content.

**Primetime Broadcast Shows with Violent Content**
**Aired 8-10pm**

| DAY | PROGRAM (NETWORK) |
|---|---|
| Monday | 24 (FOX)<br>International Fighting League – Battleground (MY Network)<br>Prison Break (FOX) |
| Tuesday | American Heiress (MY Network)<br>Law & Order: Criminal Intent (NBC)<br>NCIS (CBS)<br>The Unit (CBS) |
| Wednesday | Bones (FOX)<br>Criminal Minds (CBS)<br>Crossing Jordan (NBC)<br>Saints and Sinners (MY Network) |
| Thursday | CSI (CBS)<br>Grey's Anatomy (ABC) |
| Friday | Close to Home (CBS)<br>Ghost Whisperer (CBS)<br>Grey's Anatomy (ABC)<br>Raines (NBC)<br>Smallville CW)<br>Supernatural (CW) |
| Saturday | Cops (FOX)<br>America's<br>Law & Order (NBC)<br>Most Wanted (FOX)<br>WWE Smackdown (CW) |
| Sunday | Cold Case (CBS)<br>Desperate Housewives (ABC) |

The problem with this *Report* we are presenting to Congress is that it is not clear from reading it which if any primetime shows are being recommended for regulation. Are we saying Law and Order should be banned during hours when children are watching? It is anyone's guess after reading this *Report*. The *Report* is not a model of clarity.

Like most parents with adolescent children, I live in perpetual fear of the shows *and* commercials to which my son or daughter will be exposed to on any given evening. Whether it is a primetime show with a violent scene or merely a commercial with a violent preview, inappropriate material pops up much too often for my comfort. I am sure my children are not the only ones who have difficulty sleeping after they are inadvertently exposed to violence on television.

I fully understand that it is my choice to turn the television on or off, and similarly, it is the viewing public's responsibility to refrain from watching shows that they consider objectionable or harmful to their families and children. Sometimes, though, it is a trailer for a news show or a promotion for a horror movie that comes on during what was considered safe family programming, like the Super Bowl. As a parent and policymaker, I am profoundly concerned by the general lack of accountability, compassion, and thoughtfulness of some in the media entertainment industry. Yet this *Report* offers no discussion or suggestions as to what to do about violence in advertising and promotional spots during shows when children are watching, which is one of the biggest complaints we hear from parents in the real world. At a minimum, this is an issue worth confronting through a public-private partnership with the major media outlets.

Studies have shown, and my personal observations support, that by age 18, an American child will have seen upwards of 15,000 simulated murders and about 200,000 acts of violence. Clearly, there is something wrong with this picture. Government has an important role to support parents who are struggling to protect the well-being of their children.

Borne out of this concern and responsibility, over three years ago, the Committee on Energy and Commerce of the U.S. House of Representatives sent a letter requesting that the Commission study media violence and its impact upon children. The Committee asked the Commission to formulate and propose a definition of "excessively violent programming" that would be able to withstand constitutional scrutiny. Specifically, the Committee wanted the Commission to analyze "whether there are any constitutional limitations in defining 'excessively violent programming that is harmful to children,' or in constraining or prohibiting broadcast of such material during hours when children are likely to be a significant part of the broadcast viewing audience." The Commission further asked for "measures that [could] facilitate a consumer's use of the television rating system."

This *Report* is part of a national dialogue between the American people, Congress, regulatory agencies, public interest organizations, the courts and the entertainment industry. In light of this national interest, this *Report* should include an objective, authoritative discussion of the constitutional and regulatory challenges of regulating media content based on our experience with regulating indecent speech. The *Report* should provide a complete and thorough analysis of all parental control technologies and resources that are currently available to families and households. Overall, this *Report* should weigh the national interest of protecting children from violent content against the cumulative effect of all available parental control technologies and resources, and the constitutional concerns. It should provide a working definition most likely to sustain judicial scrutiny. In so doing, the *Report* should make recommendations that would empower parents and families, and provide Congress with a set of options – not just content and price regulation. In short, the Report should do what Congress asked.

To my disappointment, this *Report* does not fully display the experience and informed judgment of an expert federal agency that has regulated media content over thirty years. Specifically, this Report does not deal adequately with the constitutional dimensions of regulating violent content on free over-the-air TV, or subscription-based cable and satellite TV services. In fact, it muddies the issues and legal distinctions that the courts have made regarding the ability of the government to intervene in different media formats. Nor does this Report discuss fully how federal courts have ruled in numerous cases involving the regulation of violence. Oddly enough, the Report does not even discuss the full menu of parental assistance tools that are available today to millions of families. And, as a result of this incomplete analysis, the recommendations made in this Report are not fully responsive to the specific questions presented by the Committee, or inadequate to provide parents, like me, with the necessary support to protect our children. Like a financial consultant who advises a client that he could win the lottery, this *Report* discusses an optimal conclusion, but does not provide a complete analysis or a sound plan.

Congress asked the Commission to study media violence and to propose a definition of violence that would be "best suited, and most likely to be sustained in court." Rather than acknowledge that, after three years, the Commission has been unable to so, the *Report* passes the buck, declaring that "Congress could do so." The definitional difficulties here should not be dealt with in such a casual, dismissive manner. After all, this is a protected constitutional right under the First Amendment that we are recommending Congress to curtail without any thoughtful legal analysis. We shirk our responsibility by saying that we can define violence that should be banned since the guidelines developed by the television industry contain categories of violence for ratings purposes. Which of those categories do we propose to ban during hours when children are watching? Given that we are not able to offer a definition ourselves, it does not appear to be as easy to define as some suggest.

The fact of the matter is that "not all violence is created equal."[2] The Commission has not been able to formulate and recommend a definition of violence that would cover the majority of violent content that is inappropriate for children, provide fair guidance to programmers, and stand a decent chance of withstanding constitutional scrutiny, in light of judicial precedent. While we may want to define prohibited-violence and regulate it in conformance with constitutional standards, the *Report* does not refer to any court or judicial scholar that has suggested such definition is available or probable.

To the contrary, the *Report* diminishes the extent to which courts have either expressed serious skepticism or invalidated efforts to regulate violent content.[3] I believe we have an obligation to provide Congress with the complete analysis of this "jurisprudential quagmire," whereby "any regulation of television violence confronts an inherent tradeoff between precision and effectiveness" and "any restriction in this area that is neither overboard nor vague will leave unregulated so much violent programming that it will no longer accomplish a compelling interest."[4]

The central tension we face is that adults' access to violent programming is protected under the First Amendment to the U.S. Constitution. The difficult question is precisely which violent programming, if any, the government can regulate in the interest of protecting children. That question – the most challenging Congress faces – is never answered here.

Providing Congress with a complete record should be the central objective of this *Report*, but sadly that is not accomplished. In 2003, the Commission found that "new modes of media have transformed the landscape, providing more choice, greater flexibility, and more control than at any other time in history." In today's *Report,* however, the Commission simply ignores many of the developments that empower parents and viewers with more control over their programming choices. Cable subscribers, for example, have various options available, depending on if they have digital or analog cable. Digital cable set-top boxes allow parents to block shows with certain ratings, titles, or by time or date, and analog cable subscribers can use their set-top or "lockbox" technology that locks specific channels so that channel can no longer be viewed. Digital and personal video recorders, and video-on-demand permit families to "time-shift" or watch programming whenever they deem appropriate. Similarly, satellite TV subscribers have access to the Locks & Limits feature on DirecTV and Adult Guard on Dish Network. In addition to these operator-provided control technologies, TV manufacturers have been required since 1997 to install a V-Chip in all TV sets larger than 13 inches, giving parents the ability to block certain content based on age- and content-based rating. Parents and viewers may find that these tools provide varying degrees of effectiveness but this *Report* fails to explore these issues adequately.

The Commission is justifiably concerned about the limited consumer use of the V-Chip, the limited consumer understanding of the rating system and the limited deployment of digital cable set-top boxes and their accompanying advanced parental control features. However, these tools – and the online resources – provide a good basis from which to build. Instead of rushing to conclude that the TV ratings

---

[2] UCLA Center for Communication Policy, The UCLA Television Violence Report 1997.

[3] *Winters v. New York*, 333 U.S. 507, 510-11 (1948); *Interactive Digital Software Assoc. v. St Louis County*, 329 F.3d 954 (8th Cir. 2003); *American Amusement Machine Ass'n v. Kendrick*, 244 F.3d 572 (7th Cir 2001), *cert denied*, 122 S.Ct. 462 (2001); *Eclipse Enters. v. Gulotta*, 134 F.3d 63 (2nd Cir. 1997); *Video Software Dealer's Ass'n v. Webster*, 968 F.2d 684 (8th Cir. 1992); Allied Artists Pictures Corp. v. Alford, 410 F. Supp. 1348 (W.D. Tenn 1976).

[4] Harry T. Edwards and Mitchell N. Berman, *Regulating Violence on Television*, 89 NORTHWESTERN U.L. REV. 1487, 1502-03, 1555 (1995).

system – whether voluntary or mandatory – is and will always likely be unworkable, and that blocking technology does not adequately promote parental supervision and protect the well-being of children, the Commission has an obligation to advise Congress how we can attempt to improve their effectiveness. We fail to do so here.

While this *Report* recommends content and price regulation as the only legislative remedies to address violence on TV, I believe the Commission is missing a historic opportunity to discuss a host of meaningful "consumer choice" recommendations that would truly enhance and facilitate parents' effort to safeguard their children from the exposure to violent programming. From developing enforceable public interest obligations to implementing a national consumer education campaign, there are other recommendations that should be part of the national dialogue on media violence.

If we were able to craft a constitutionally-sustainable definition of violence, presumably it would apply to only the most extreme and gratuitous depictions of violence. While that might help parents navigate past a few icebergs in a sea of violence, they would still be faced with sailing a pretty stormy sea on their own. Our own experience in regulating indecency demonstrates that regulation only applies to the most egregious cases, and there is a vast array of sexually explicit television that many parents, including myself, would find inappropriate for their children but which does not rise to the level of indecency. In the case of violence, I certainly would not want my children watching the opening scenes of *Saving Private Ryan*, but I doubt any court would uphold us banning it during evening hours. I do not even like my kids watching a cartoon of an anvil falling on the coyote's head, but I do not think any court would let us ban it. So our narrowly focused recommendations might help on the margins, but do little to deal with the vast problem parents confront on a daily basis.

One of our few recommendations, a la carte, which is primarily a price-regulation mechanism, is far too blunt an instrument to provide much help to beleaguered parents who already have the ability to block any cable channel they want, whether they are analog or digital subscribers. The History Channel, for example, sometimes broadcasts war scenes far too violent for young children, but dropping it would deprive them of valuable educational content it often airs. TV violence is not viewed in the record as a channel-by-channel problem. Perhaps that is why leading experts have not suggested a la carte as a solution. It makes its debut here with little explanation as to why or how it would be of any practical use to parents.

Given how much of the concern about violence arises from what is on broadcast television, it is not even clear how a la carte price regulation would help parents avoid violent programming unless it applied to each broadcast channel, which this report does nothing to clarify. I suppose a parent could choose to receive only Home and Garden Television and the Food Channel to avoid violent programming, since there are so few other channels devoid of violence, but I do not see how that helps parents much.

A recent study from the Parents Television Council (PTC) found that, in midst of the unprecedented wave of media consolidation between 1998 and 2006, violence on television during the hours of 8:00 p.m., 9 p.m. and 10 p.m. grew by 45, 92 and 167 percent, respectively.[5] This finding is highly relevant to the Commission's current review of the broadcast media ownership rules. The apparent correlation between increased media concentration and media violence questions whether *any* effort to permit further concentration of ownership can be squared with the public interest. Furthermore, this finding reinforces the substantial need of Congress and/or this Commission to develop enforceable public

---

[5] *Dying to Entertain: Violence on Prime Time Broadcast Television 1998 to 2006,* Parents Television Council, Special Report, January 2007, at 6.

interests obligations for general audience broadcast programming.[6] Despite repeated requests from Members of Congress, consumer and children's advocacy organizations, Commissioner Copps and me, this Commission has failed to complete a proceeding to address this important concern since 1999.

So while this *Report* focuses its recommendations on the novel and questionable approach of mandating a la carte, and constitutionally-difficult content regulation, it neglects to provide much discussion of a host of tools that could clearly provide parents some relief. Rather than focusing solely on the sliver of violent programming that may or may not be amenable to regulation, we should have also focused on the real, everyday problems parents face which are more fully addressed by more comprehensive solutions that sometimes involve working with media executives to set better standards to protect children from exposure to TV violence.

Other recommendations that do not implicate constitutional protections, but are noticeably missing from this Report, include the need for a coordinated and sustained national effort to educate parents, engage industry and encourage the development of new technologies. Such an effort could include an education campaign, authorized and funded by Congress, would seek to improve consumer awareness and understanding of all existing parental controls technologies and resources, especially the V-Chip and content descriptors. A multi-faceted campaign would: (1) expand existing industry-led and private efforts, such as TVboss.org. and Pause Parent Play, to further educate parents and families; (2) require manufacturers set new TVs to receive only TV-G children programming, until consumers and parents reset or opt-in for programming that is appropriate for their household; (3) rate all programming, including news, promotions and commercials;[7] (4) use audio, in addition to visual, ratings and descriptors of all rated programs; (5) promote media literacy at schools; (6) encourage more positive children's programming; and (7) encourage the development of enhanced V-Chip software and blocking technologies to filter objectionable content.

Congress could also consider legislation that explicitly exempts a television code and a family hour from antitrust law. This measure could permit the broadcast, cable, satellite and advertising industries to establish an inter-industry code on the subject of television violence. Such an approach, along with the national coordinated effort and education campaign, I believe, would help reduce children's exposure to media violence. Accordingly, these ideas deserve consideration by Congress, even though they are not mentioned in this Report.

Unfortunately for those who care passionately about this issue, as I certainly do, this Report could do much more. I vote for it because it is a start and better than nothing, but we leave much of the real work to Congress to tackle the tough issues Congress asked us to help them with.

---

[6] As the Supreme Court has held, and this Commission has argued passionately in court, "a licensed broadcaster is 'granted the free and exclusive use of a limited and valuable part of the public domain; when he accepts that franchise it is burdened by enforceable public obligations.'" *CBS v. FCC*, 453 U.S. 367, 388 (1969).

[7] A 2004 study of commercials during major sporting events found that almost one in five displayed behavior deemed unsafe or violent, and, as a result, urged parents to limit and supervise their children exposure to televised sports. See Robert F. Tamburro, Patricia L. Gordon, James P. D'Apolito and Scott C. Howard, *Unsafe and Violent Behavior in Commercials Aired During Televised Major Sporting Events*, 114 Pediatrics (Dec 2004), at 694-698.

## STATEMENT OF
## COMMISSIONER DEBORAH TAYLOR TATE

*Re: In the Matter of Violent Television Programming and Its Impact on Children,* **MB Docket No. 04-261**

Members of Congress requested the FCC launch an inquiry regarding negative effects of violent programming, the constitutional limitations on restricting violent programming when children are likely to be viewing, and the constitutionality and public interest basis for adopting a definition of "excessively violent programming that is harmful to children." While I recognize the difficulty in drafting narrowly tailored and constitutionally sustainable definitions in this matter, after reviewing the studies and meeting with researchers and those who have been involved in this debate for decades, I am convinced that something must be done to help parents minimize the pernicious effects of violent programming on their children. Congress faces difficult issues everyday and constantly walks a tight constitutional line, but, as Albert Einstein once said, "In the middle of difficulty lies opportunity."

Like many of the parents, experts and health professionals we heard from, I am deeply concerned about the negative effects violent programming appears to have on our children. Many of us, as parents, have witnessed our children acting out a fighting scene from an episode of Teenage Mutant Ninja Turtles, been shocked by our children's callousness towards violence, or been awakened by a frightened child climbing into bed after having a nightmare because of something they saw on television. While the Report we submit to Congress today recognizes that there is some research refuting the causal relationship between violent programming and aggressive behavior, the vast majority of studies indicate that violent programming does have a negative impact – ranging from increased desensitization to violence to sleep abnormalities to heightened fears of becoming a victim – on children. I'm sure the 81 percent of parents who believe that violence on television contributes to violent behavior in children will agree with many of our findings.

The debate regarding the impact of violent programming is not a new one. In fact, it made its official debut in 1952 with the first Congressional hearing on the matter. The discussions, the political rhetoric, the hearings, and indeed the promises made by the industry during those hearings have been remade, rehashed, reinvented, and recycled in the following 55 years. While I support self-regulation first, these discussions have been going on for far too long. It is time that more effective steps are taken to protect our children.

Following the passage of the 1996 Communications Act, countless parents and advocacy groups, the FCC, and indeed Congress strongly encouraged the industry to adopt a "ratings system." Today, we have an age-based system with general content descriptors warning of violence, language, sexual situations, and suggestive dialogue.

While this was a positive, *voluntary* industry step, it has proven to be insufficient to protect our children. Individual networks rate each of their programs, leading to inconsistencies across channels, and even across shows. Age-based ratings may reasonably reflect the content of the shows, but content descriptors frequently are not used or would be considered inaccurate by an impartial observer. For example, a program may very well have violent content, but if the network does not believe it constitutes "moderate" violence, a "V" label is not applied. The industry also frequently labels intense violence in children's programs as "FV," for comedic violence or fantasy violence, regardless of whether it is fantasy or realistic, merely because it appears in children's programming. Yet, research shows that children aged 7 and younger often perceive fantasy or comedic violence as reality.

The industry should implement ratings reliably, more completely, consistently, and accurately. A properly implemented ratings system would be a very useful tool for parents when used together with the V-Chip. Unfortunately, notwithstanding government and industry educational efforts, more than half of Americans do not know their television is equipped with a V-Chip and two-thirds have never used it. Thus, effectively educating parents about the V-Chip is an additional necessary step. Further, our report notes that the industry could voluntarily commit itself to reducing the amount of excessive violence viewed by our children. A good first step would be to readopt a family hour during which there is no violent content, period.

Over the past few years, sources from outside the industry have introduced new tools and technology designed to help parents make smart choices about what kind of violent content is age-appropriate and available to children. For example:

- Parents Television Council provides on its web site a rating of a significant number of network programs based on PTC employees' log of every instance of violence, language, sexual situation, and suggestive dialogue.

- Common Sense Media has rated more than 6,000 media titles from a kids and family perspective – including violent content ratings. These reviews are distributed not just through Common Sense's website, but also through major Internet and cable partners such as Comcast, Time Warner Cable, and Road Runner High Speed.

- TV Guardian technology actually detects and filters profanity and other offensive phrases chosen by the parent – including "hate words" and racial slurs – while you watch movies or television shows.

While independent information can facilitate parental control, in today's 24/7 media environment, parents need more help. Our Report concludes that the available tools and technological "fixes" are not sufficient to protect our children from violent programming. There is no doubt that parents are the ones who know their children best, and are the first line of defense in keeping their kids from viewing violent content they aren't ready to see. But both the industry and the government have an important role to play: in educating the public about the problem as well as potential solutions; in encouraging the development of more and better tools; in brokering partnerships so that parents have better access to accurate information; and in listening to both experts and parents across this country. I pledge my assistance in these efforts.

I will close with this thought: we, parents, must take responsibility for the media that is viewed *inside* our homes, but also must be active in changing the media landscape *outside* our homes. I encourage all parents to let your local TV station know when something you find inappropriate is aired, and be sure to notify your representatives in Congress. If enough parents speak out, perhaps we will not only improve the tools that are available to parents to help minimize their children's exposure to violent content, but we will actually see an increase in the amount of family-friendly, uplifting and nonviolent programming being produced.

## STATEMENT OF
## COMMISSIONER ROBERT M. MCDOWELL

*Re:*     *In the Matter of Violent Television Programming and Its Impact on Children,* **Report to**
          **Congress**

As the father of three young children, I am deeply concerned about the coarsening of television content and the effects of television violence on children. As a society, we should do all that the law allows to help shield our children from harmful television content. Today's Report is a response to Congress' 2004 request that the FCC provide a comprehensive summary and analysis of the factual and legal landscape surrounding this issue. Although I would have preferred a more thorough study, I support this Report as a well-intentioned, if not complete, first step toward launching a new national dialogue on this important matter. The Report provides a helpful summary of the social science research regarding the effects of exposure to violence in the media on the behavior of children. It provides a preliminary discussion of the effectiveness of the TV ratings system and blocking technologies and of the issues regarding how government may define violence for regulatory purposes.

Congress may wish to build upon what the Commission has started by digging deeper into the issues we raise today. For instance, further discussion should probe into many areas by better researching the answers to many important questions, including:

- What additional actions can parents take to protect their children?
- How can industry and government help educate parents regarding their options?
- How effective are screening and content selection technologies that are currently available to families? and
- What constitutional challenges lie ahead should Congress and the Commission decide to enact and implement a new anti-violence regime?

In my view, the next step should be to review fully the screening and content selection tools parents currently have and find ways that industry and government can help educate parents regarding those options. Parents should be the first and last line of defense in protecting their children from excessively violent content, or any other content that may cause harm to children. Unfortunately, today's Report does not sufficiently brief Congress on the full range of tools available or what can be done to mobilize parents in this pursuit. I hope that our Report does not lull some into thinking that government action alone is the answer to the television violence pandemic. By itself, government action would be an insufficient cure. Even if Congress were able to enact flawlessly worded legislation that enjoyed perfect enforcement, parents play the most important role in deciding what is appropriate for their families. While government can and should do all that it can to protect children, parents should not shirk their primary responsibility to be actively engaged in their upbringing.

Fortunately, today's parents have at their disposal more choices in parental controls and blocking technologies than ever before. Never have parents been more empowered to choose what their children should and should not watch. Since January 2000, as required by Congress, all TV sets with screens 13 inches or larger come equipped with the V-chip, which allows parents to block programs based on the TV rating assigned to those programs. Cable operators provide parental controls in both their analog and digital set-top boxes, with more advanced controls in the digital boxes. DBS subscribers have access to parental controls that allow blocking by channel, by program, by time and/or by TV rating. Tivo offers KidsZone, a tool that combines editorial recommendations from experts with technology for parents to select the shows they want their children to watch. Moreover, all consumers have an unprecedented amount of control over what they watch and when they watch it through DVDs, programs that are downloadable from websites and through time-shifting technologies such as digital video recorders.

As discussed in the Report, however, research has shown that while the vast majority of parents are concerned about violent content on TV, very few of them use most parental controls. It seems that many parents do not have sufficient knowledge about these technologies, and about the TV ratings system, to use parental controls effectively. Industry and government should encourage additional consumer education so that parents can learn about the tools available to them. Campaigns aimed at educating parents, such as thetvboss.org and pauseparentplay.org, are a great start. Their websites provide detailed practical information about the V-chip, cable and satellite controls and TV ratings, among other things. Also, groups like Common Sense Media and the Parents Television Council offer reviews of TV shows and movies to help provide guidance to parents. More needs to be done, however, to make a connection between parental concerns about content inappropriate for their children and parental use of tools that will help them make and enforce their programming choices. I strongly encourage the private sector and public interest groups to continue their work in this pursuit.

Meanwhile, even though the market is developing and promoting technological solutions that may help parents control the television content that their children view, Congress still may deem it necessary to place statutory restrictions on the broadcast of excessively violent content. The Commission would be remiss if it did not underscore to Congress that such a voyage, although noble in its goal, will lead us through uncharted constitutional waters. I am disappointed that this Report does not provide more than a cursory mention of these important legal issues. It fails to illuminate a path for Congress to follow in order to safely avoid what legal pitfalls may lie ahead. Should Congress pursue the laudable endeavor of protecting America's children from excessive television violence through new statutory mandates, it should first take the step of seeking additional constitutional legal advice. Any action should be conducted in a prudent manner that withstands constitutional muster. The 39 House members who directed us to conduct our inquiry demanded as much when they asked the Commission specifically to address in this Report the "constitutional limitations" in defining "excessively violent programming that is harmful to children" or in "constraining or prohibiting broadcast of such material during hours when children are likely to be a significant or part of the broadcast viewing audience." I fear that our Report may fall short of their request.

Additionally, this Report briefly outlines court decisions upholding the Commission's authority to regulate the broadcast of indecent content by restricting the airing of such content during certain hours. I note that the brief constitutional discussion in the Report focuses solely on the regulation of <u>broadcast</u> television. Other possible mandates mentioned in the Report, such as requiring MVPDs to provide channels on family tiers or on an à la carte basis, would require the regulation of non-broadcast entities, possibly cable operators, DBS providers and other MVPDs. Accordingly, before Congress adopts any of these possible mandates, I suggest that Congress seek analysis of such regulation under the applicable constitutional standard. Potential Congressional action against television violence based upon our Report should only be considered in the limited context of broadcasting because the Commission has not offered sufficient legal analysis to support broader regulation.

In sum, I support this Report and hope that it is helpful to Congress. This is only the first step in what I hope will be a comprehensive study of governmental options to inform the national debate over television violence. The governmental interest at stake – protecting children from excessively violent television programming – is powerful, of course. Nonetheless, historically, courts have balanced similar interests against the First Amendment rights of broadcasters with mixed results. As our experience with the indecency laws has shown, enforcement of such regulations involves the difficult task of defining the inappropriate content and then applying that definition in the context of specific programming. Defining excessive violence in a legally sustainable way and applying that definition will be at least as difficult. As recent tragedies have reminded us, we live in an often violent world. News reports, documentaries and other television programs must address violent topics, almost by necessity, which makes defining excessive violence that much more difficult. While we should encourage Congress' further examination of this issue, having a new statutory regime regulating television violence overturned by the courts on constitutional grounds only would undermine the very crusade against television violence that any prospective legislation may intend to address. Such a defeat could set back the cause for years. In the meantime, as a society, we should do all that we can to achieve our goal through all available means. Our children deserve no less.

www.ingramcontent.com/pod-product-compliance
Lightning Source LLC
Chambersburg PA
CBHW080639290526

45790CB00007B/3132